THE LAST CHANCE FISHING CLUB

and other stories

STEVEN MURGATROYD

First Edition, published 2022 by

The Fishingcane Press

ISBN: 9781916596177

Editor/designer: **Nicholas J. Murgatroyd**

www.thelastchancefishingclub.net

About the author

Steven Murgatroyd has been a fanatical fisherman for over fifty years. These days he fishes almost exclusively with the fly rod; eagerly pursuing game, coarse and saltwater species. He also enjoys listening to music and documenting his various piscine escapades, resulting in his first book.

His writing has been featured in a variety of well-known fishing-related print and digital publications, having won various awards including first prize in the Balvenie 'Story to Tell' competition, the Grayling Society Righyni-Roose Award for excellence in the written word, and first place in the *Fish and Fly* writing competition.

He is a trustee of The Wild Carp Trust and a life member of The Wild Trout Trust.

He lives on the Welsh borders with his family. At the bottom of the garden, conveniently enough, is a trout stream…

<u>Acknowledgements</u>

A mixture of old and new writing – some fact, some fiction; some fact *and* fiction - comprises this collection. Most of what you're about to read originally appeared at one time or another in magazines and periodicals such as *Fly Fishing & Fly Tying*, *Fly Culture*, *Trout and Salmon*, *Flydresser* and *Grayling*. My grateful thanks to the respective editors of said publications (particularly Mark Bowler and Pete Tyjas), including any I've neglected to mention, for granting me permission to collect and reproduce my work for the purposes of this book. Acknowledgement also goes to Richard Holman of John French Rods; with my gratitude not only for his friendship (and guidance on bamboo rods!), but also for contributing what I consider the better parts of *"A Rod of Distinction."*

Important mentions are also due my fellow members of the Flyfishers' Club, particularly Nigel 'Fennel' Hudson - for his friendship and inspiration - as well as Matthew Wright, who introduced me to the club, resulting in my being able to connect with so many kind and generous *"brothers of the angle"*.

Particular thanks to my parents for encouraging my fishy pursuits as a child; my wife Lesley for putting up with my obsession and subsequent regular absences; my daughter Victoria, who I feel truly understands my fanaticism and, last but not least, my son Nick, for his assistance and valuable input with regard to the editing and overall design of the book.

All stories originally appeared in *Fly Fishing and Fly Tying* magazine, other than "A GOOD PLACE", "FLY RODS, WHISKY AND WILD, WILD TROUT", "THE NON-SMOKER'S GUIDE TO CATCHING MORE TROUT" & "A ROD OF DISTINCTION," which originally appeared in *Fly Culture* magazine, and "THE STALKER" which was featured in *Trout and Salmon*. All remaining pieces originally appeared on *Eat, Sleep, Fish*, or in *Flydresser* or *Grayling*.

Prefatory Note...

The eagle-eyed reader will no doubt notice some degree of repetition within the pages of this book. Virtually all pieces, respectively, were written for an array of fishing-themed publications over the course of twenty-or-so years. Consequently, a certain amount of duplication here and there is, perhaps, an inevitability. In the spirit of completeness and presenting each piece as organically as possible (or 'as-intended'), such instances of this will not necessarily have been amended...

I hope you will not find these minor repetitive instances *too* distracting! The following stories do not appear in any particular order other than the first and last, which I feel serve to 'book-end' the collection nicely.

-- Steven Murgatroyd

To the water, the fish, the earth…

TABLE OF CONTENTS

"Be Careful What You Wish For!"

Cartoon by Nicholas Murgatroyd

Fishy Beginnings

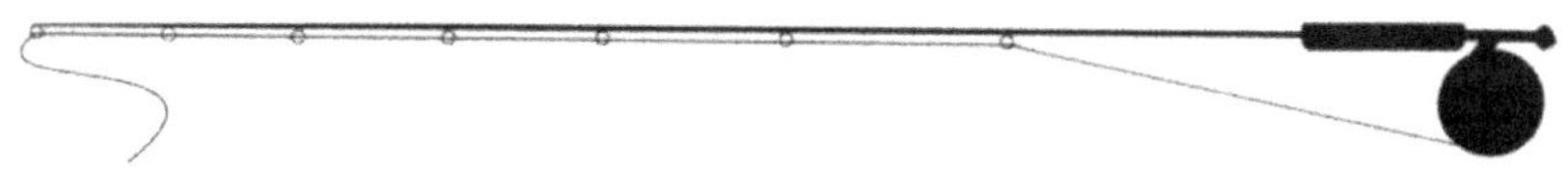

The fish was big.

I was small.

It did what only fish can do: without any obvious movement, it began a slow-motion fade…

It took me a moment to realise that, empty-headed, I was staring at empty water. Could I really have seen such a beautiful thing? Or was it just a daydream - a trick of the light, a flick of the tail?

Now, at fifty-something, I can still see that watery jewel. Teasing me. Tempting me… just as it did on that sixties' summer's day when, net in hand, a tadpole-hunter became a fisherman…

A Constant Star

Abrief glimpse of a fish in a tiny pond, more debris than water...

That, I'm pretty sure, was the beginning of it all. My parents didn't fish, although they *did* encourage and indulge my new interest. My grandparents didn't fish and, being an only child, I had no siblings who fished either! But it must have come from somewhere, and I'm sure it was that brief glimpse into another world (my own personal Narnia or Wonderland) that did it, capturing me for life - making me a willing prisoner of my own addiction. And it *is* an addiction. An obsession which, at times, can fill every waking moment. Even spilling over into sleep; fuelling evermore ambitious dreams – spiralling out of control, more often than not - firing the imagination and resulting in madcap forays in pursuit of the uncatchable. Dreams destined for failure and frustration.

But this isn't the failure and frustration that grows from the daily grind; the insidious despair that life in general can cultivate within your soul. It is, in fact, the very opposite. Dreams are important; very important. We soon learn there are no false promises to be had in the pursuit of our quarry. Nature offers no guarantees. But that is its attraction. There are so many variables that success is never a given. Persistence, however, will eventually be rewarded. The day *will* dawn when the weather is perfect, the water is perfect, the fish are feeding on flies you can actually see *and* match - and your casting ability is not tested too much. The dream will eventually be realised. And this train of thought, I believe, is why I keep returning...

It doesn't take long to discover that life can be pretty disappointing and unpleasant at times. On a global level, war, poverty and crime prove themselves beyond the control of democracy. While on a personal level, 'the three D's' - death, divorce and debt – often conspire to drive people to drink or despair. There is even anecdotal evidence to suggest that in the very worst cases, certain individuals have even sought solace in golf.

But one thing of which I am certain is that fly fishing - for all its variables - has proved to be the one constant in my life. Something I can return to again and again. Certain in the knowledge that, whatever else life may cast my way, I can always rely on the rivers, lakes and streams; their inhabitants and their surroundings - to refresh and replenish my soul in a way nothing else can. In an ever-changing world, fly fishing has been my guiding, constant star.

Black Crow Blues

With a nod to Jim Dodge*, I had loaded the CD stacker with Dylan, the Stones and 'Van The Man.' Fuelled by the cinematic romance of the American road trip, we had planned our own pioneering adventure to the wild west (Anglesey), in search of bass on the fly. As the music rang out, I tried, in my mind's eye, to morph the A61 into Highway 61. I struggled.

There were few cars on the road and, for mile after mile, the only signs of life were the lonely sheep and the numerous death-black carrion crows that, sensing our approach, lifted as one from the lonely road.

"Stop!" screamed Wilbury. All the gear in the back of the Land Rover lurched forward as the brakes took hold. "Look at all this road kill. Let's collect some of it and drop it off at "Pete the Gaff"'s place! He might point us in the right direction to find the fish." Apparently, 'Pete the Gaff' has lobster pots and uses road kill for bait. As for his nickname, Wilbury said it would all become clear once I met him.

The crows became less fearful and increasingly belligerent and vocal as we scraped the stinking roadkill into an old carrier bag, which we then secured to the roof rack. As we pulled away, I glanced in the mirror and watched as a huge flock of crows rose like a swarm of flies to follow us — just as gulls might follow a fishing boat.

Pete's place was a small, stone-built cottage that, like its owner, had seen better days. As we pulled up, he was loading his pots onto the back of a rusting flat-bed truck. Where his left hand had been there was now a brass coloured hook, the legacy of a biking accident. The hook, although not as dextrous as a hand, was at least of some use to a man who makes his living hauling pots out of the Irish Sea. We exchanged tentative nods before he disappeared into the dark recesses of his cottage with Wilbury to examine the road kill.

I circled around the Land Rover, kicking at the tyres and trying not to feel too self-conscious. The cottage was surrounded by a tangle of stunted oak trees, and I suddenly had the feeling I was being watched; that I was not alone. As I turned, intending to go into the cottage to find Wilbury, Pete loomed into view. He turned his attention to the vehicle and all the gear. Studying the tent and sleeping bags, he said, "I hope you guys are married."

"Yes, we are," I replied, and then hastily added, "but not to each other." There was an awkward silence I felt compelled to break. "Why?" I asked.

"Because if you're serious about catching bass with a fly, then you need to have experienced regular disappointment and rejection." Smiling, he turned back towards the cottage, the noise of the birds in the trees growing louder.

Back on the road, Wilbury navigated our way to the rocky headland which Pete had suggested we might try. The sky was now dark and low. Rain-filled clouds, the colour of bruises, threatened to burst at any moment. All the time flocks of crows, and now gulls, tormented the already agitated air with their mocking cries.

We fished hard for a while, knowing the conditions were hopeless. Wilbury took a biscuit out of his pocket and unwrapped it. As he went to take a bite, a bird pounced on him, knocking off his hat, which the wind then grabbed and tossed toward the sea. Instinctively, Wilbury lunged at the hat and I watched in horror as he lost his footing and tumbled off the ledge and into the sea! Somehow, he held on to his rod and I managed to grab the tip and inch him back on to the rocks as the swell elevated him. We didn't have to say it — we both knew we were defeated. We made our way back to the Land Rover...

On the journey home, we pulled into a lay-by on a high and lonely Pennine road. Still the crows were omnipresent, the sky threatening, and road kill littered the carriageway. As we ate and drank, I could not take my eyes off the mirror. Through the rear window, I watched in disbelief as three crows herded a young rabbit to the edge of the road. They held it in position just as a dog might shepherd a sheep. The rabbit's eyes were wide with fear. I suddenly became aware of the distant sound of an approaching car. The birds became more alert and tensed themselves, their heads cocked to one side as they listened. The staring rabbit trembled. The engine noise grew louder — now competing with the wind and the incessant cawing. Suddenly, the car was upon us and the crows, with a final, deadly flourish forced the rabbit into the road and beneath its wheels.

As I turned away, a crow thumped down on to the nearside wing mirror and tested the glass of the windscreen with its beak. With its cold, lifeless eyes, it studied Wilbury and I. As life imitated art in that cold, desolate place, I nor Wilbury remained convinced that our position at the top of the food chain was as secure as we had believed it to be...

* *'Rain on the River'* by Jim Dodge. Published by Cannongate

Got My Mojo Working...

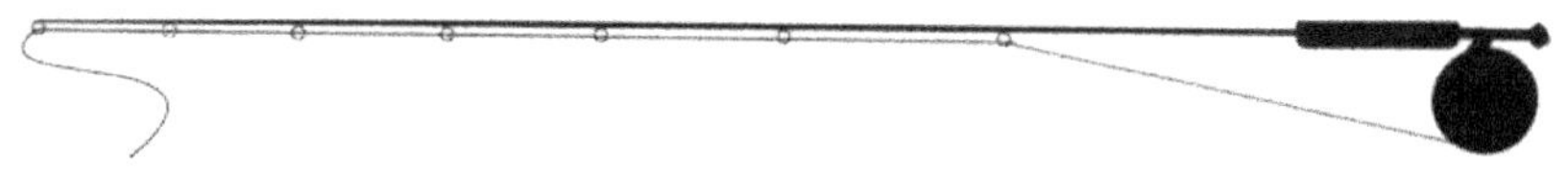

"Any luck?", is the usual greeting; following which a rather tedious question-and-answer session takes place...

"Caught anything, then?"

"Some."

"What?"

"Fish, err... trout, I mean... erm..."

"How many?" I force a smile.

"A couple."

"How big?"

"Oh, not too bad..."

And at some point, the inevitable *"I don't have the patience for fishing"* will be thrown into the conversation with just enough condescension to make it clear that what they really mean is that they can't believe anybody could be so stupid as to spend their precious time in such an absurd way.

All the time they've been talking, their children/dog(s) will have been given free rein to cause such a commotion that any life form of note in the immediate vicinity will have vacated the area for the foreseeable future. The encounter usually ends with "Good luck!" Do they not realise it is *skill* - not luck - that brings success? Although luck is what you're *going* to need if you have any more encounters like *this* today! It is kind of interesting, however, that most non-anglers seem to assume that luck plays a significant part in fishing and, on reflection, maybe they are actually on to something…

I've never really thought myself a superstitious character, tending to lean more towards the belief that the harder you work at something, the luckier you get. But now I'm beginning to think that maybe this is oversimplifying things somewhat. I guess the most powerful tool you can have in your armoury - in *any* kind of endeavour - is probably that of confidence and self-belief. Now if we look at confidence, it could be argued that it grows with experience. The more experiences you have - assuming you learn from them - the more you will develop the ability to asses a wide range of circumstances with some degree of certainty. As your success rate improves, so your confidence and self-belief will increase. You will visualise your success before it happens. And this increased self belief will bear fruit – fish, in this case… a self-fulfilling prophecy.

How many times have you just *known* you were going to catch something, even when those around you were struggling? Some like to call this a *'sixth sense'*. I used to fish with someone who claimed he could *smell* the fish in the river and, usually, he would be proved right and have very little difficulty in catching them. Literally, the sweet smell of success! Was this really a lucky sixth sense, or confidence borne of half-a-lifetime spent fishing?

Luck certainly *does* come into fishing; particularly with regard to the size of the fish we catch. Anglers are, of course, regularly parodied in the media for being obsessed with size: "It was *this* big!" or, "You should have seen the one that got away!!" Most of the anglers I know - or maybe that should be *'prefer'* to know! - would not pass up the chance to catch a 'big' fish (big being relative to the location – something not usually understood by non-anglers. *How* can anyone be excited by an eight-inch trout?!), and most accept the fact that, specimen-hunting aside, there is very little difference in the level of skill required to hook a fish, be it six ounces or six pounds! More often than not, the size difference is down to pure luck. So maybe all those dog-walking, stick-throwing, child-squawking, stone-lobbing passersby really are on to something after all... For my money, they *just might be*, and, as much as I would have promoted experience and endeavour as being key components in achieving success, I realise that I do have my own little rituals and lucky charms that play their part in every trip. I suspect, if you're being honest, that you probably have yours, too!

We all have our favourite rods and reels -- items we would hate to be without on any fishy escapade -- and should we lose or forget them, we often don't fish with our usual confidence. These lucky charms don't have to be items of tackle. One of the most common fishing charms is, of course, the fishing hat - the loss of which can signal a blight on one's fishing for some considerable time, at least until its replacement has earned its colours.

My own personal 'lucky charm' - and I know I am not alone in this - is my box of secret 'Mojo flies.' These are the flies I go to when first arriving at the water, even before there is any sign of feeding fish, or a hatch of any kind. The Mojo box is the result of years of experience: a small selection of simple flies chosen as a result of regular failure, frustration and the occasional triumph. I know that when tying one of these flies on, I'm giving myself the very best chance of success. It usually works. But only if I'm wearing the right hat. Now, is that a self-fulfilling prophecy, or just my Mojo working...?

My Latest Flame

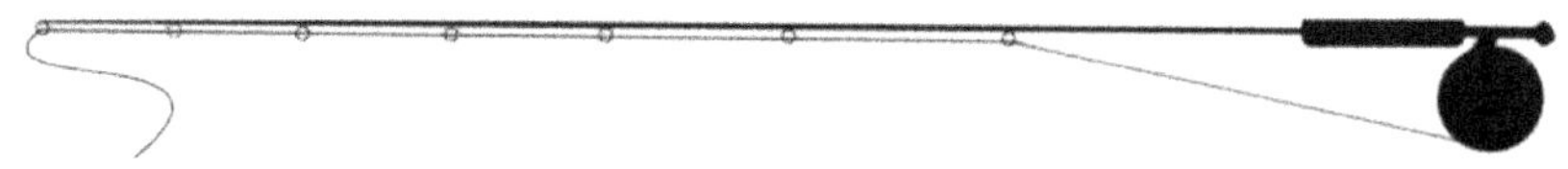

As you make your way through the gate at the bottom of the garden, you are immediately on to the riverbank. To the right is an old drovers bridge - the dull grey stone pock-marked with vivid lichens. A bright-red plaque glorifies a historic (and bloody) battle, in which the defending Welsh taught the invading English a thing or two about tactics!

Looking downstream, to the left lies the former battlefield and, across the road, "The Gate of the Dead" gives way to a steep slope of ancient woodland. Beyond those woods stands the dominating castle. The right-hand bank climbs steeply and is, again, heavily wooded. From the top of the bank is a footpath which provides an elevated, almost cinematic view of the river below. The setting is reminiscent of some of the scenes in the classic film *Deliverance*; all that seems to be missing is the sound of a banjo being played by one of the locals!

This is my "new" river. My latest flame. Her name is Ceiriog. She is now *my* river.

Technically, of course, she isn't my river at all. I actually share the several miles of fast-flowing, crystal-clear water with around eighty or so other club members - but you know what I mean. I'm sure that we all get a little territorial about our fishing spots. I admit to still experiencing a feeling of dismay when I round a bend in the stream only to discover another angler occupying *my* spot. How dare she share her secrets with another?

Still - I try to console myself with the thought that at least I'm not alone in my infatuation. Even so, sharing doesn't always come easily. It *is* possible to fish when following another angler down the stream and get some enjoyment from it. Even if it is a little like inviting a girl out on a date, only for her to turn up with her best friend. It's not *ideal.* I think what I'm trying to say is this: any fishing is better than none.

But I do have a new river - and I really do think of her as 'mine' - even after such a short courtship. I also feel a strong sense of outrage if I find that she has not been treated with the respect she deserves, that her beauty *demands.* Just give me a few minutes with those who litter her banks.

Admittedly, there *were* others before her...

My first love was the Clwyd. I was young and knew nothing, and she allowed me to learn (by trial and error) all that I thought I needed to know. And she knew, long before I did, that I would be hers.

Of course, those endless summer days were just an illusion. Before long, reality shoehorned itself into my life and, with the many distractions and frustrations that inevitably followed, there came many relocations – and as a result, a succession of rivers.

The Cheshire Dean was the next to flow through my life, followed by the Creedy in Devon.

Both small, intimate rivers that encouraged me to grow as a fisherman and practise my repertoire of skills. Then, two chalk streams: The Lambourn and The Kennet. Magnificent, demanding rivers where targeting specific and often large fish, with nymph and dry fly, became the norm. Real fun – but still, I wasn't satisfied...

A move up to Yorkshire and the Nidd turned my head and ignited my passion. I became immersed; not only in the river (which happened on several occasions) but also in the rich history and traditions of North Country fly-fishing. Little did I realise at the time that, due to my various relocations, I was enjoying a fly-fishing apprenticeship second-to-none. Enjoying, but not learning.

So, where did it all go wrong? How come I'm no better at casting or finding fish than I was at the age of twelve? Yes, I can catch fish - but I scare more than I net. Technically, I'm rubbish! Have I wasted all those opportunities on those glorious rivers that I have had the privilege of fishing? Do I *really* believe those that say they never go fishing without learning something? I wish I could believe them, but I know that I have returned from too many trips more confused than educated. Rejected and dejected, I looked for pastures new.

Perhaps it's because I have been so fickle in my affections - never putting the time and effort into building a stable and long-lasting relationship - that I have not reaped the rewards and grown as a fisherman. This time, however, I am determined that this relationship will last. This one is for keeps. The Ceiriog is mine, and I am hers. She is a beautiful river; wild, fast, and full of mystery. What more could any fisherman want?

This is one flame I *will* keep alight.

But just in case, do let me know should you hear of any other good rivers to fish. I really fancy the Itchen... or maybe the Test... or the Meon... or the Dove, or even the Eden... then there are salmon to chase in Russia, and steelhead in the States... alas...

So many rivers, so little time...

The Pringle Factor

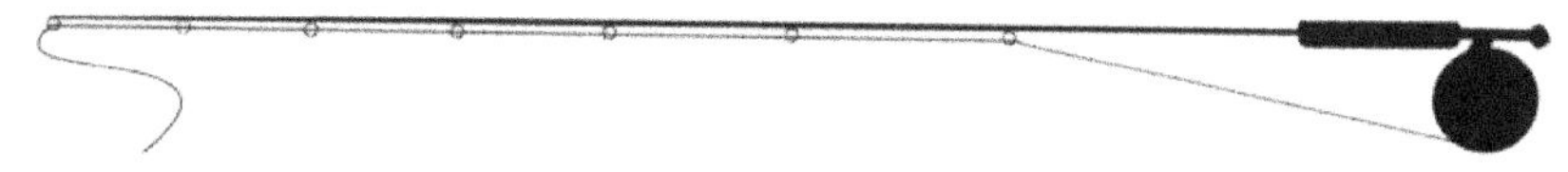

Try explaining the concept of 'the educated trout' to a non-angler and you are likely to elicit the response, "I don't think so!" Or, depending upon the age of the person you're talking to, *"Whatever!"*

For a long time, I, too, was sceptical of such a concept. If I failed to catch a fish it was because my presentation was at fault - I used to be convinced that presentation was everything. After all, surely trout, like all wild creatures, are opportunistic feeders? If something comes along that looks edible, why would they not take it? Barley, our Border Terrier, investigates everything that appears in front of him; just in case it should prove to be food. In fact, he eats a good number of things that are clearly inedible!

That said, I have gradually come to realise that the term 'educated trout' should not be used to imply a trout with a higher level of intelligence than its peers. Rather, a trout whose behaviour has become learned or imprinted, to the extent that its single-mindedness leads it to focus on specific prey items. Ignoring - or becoming blinded to - other objects that may be just as edible. The term *selective feeding* springs to mind. I don't believe this is a conscious decision made by the fish. Instead, it simply becomes "locked on" to a particular food form to the exclusion of all others. A similar style of feeling to the one *I* experience when I open a tube of Pringles (every last one *must* be eaten - even if fresh fruit is also readily available)! A trout proving difficult to catch, ignoring your offerings, is not 'educated.' It's simply being selective. All you have to do is find the fly with "The Pringle Factor" - simple!

Or maybe not… It's this frustration that leads us back to the concept of the educated trout. If we can't catch it then it *must* be endowed with some kind of of super-intelligence. After all, we don't want to admit to being outwitted by a fish! And of course, this bigging up of the fish's intellect allows us to massage our own egos when we finally do succeed in deceiving it.

Two events, however, have led me to conclude that the behaviour of human beings and trout is often very similar. In the first instance, my daughter came home from school one day with some brightly-coloured rubbery capsules containing bubble bath. She left them in a bowl on the hall table. My wife came downstairs and, upon seeing the capsules, picked one up and promptly ate it! Her only comment being that "those sweets weren't very nice - they taste really soapy!" Now, I think her behaviour was really interesting. She saw what she wanted to see. She wanted to see sweets, the capsules were the right size and colour and they smelled sweet. What Mrs. Murgatroyd was doing was behaving just like a trout ('selective' - not *old'*, I hasten to add!). She was responding to certain 'triggers'. If the triggers are there, then the detail will be ignored.

Let me give you another example: I had left my car in a busy car park. Upon returning to it, I pressed the button on the "blipper" to unlock the doors. Nothing! I tried again - still nothing. Assuming the battery must be dead, I tried the key in the lock. Again, nothing. Although the key slid into the lock without a hitch, it wouldn't turn. I tried the passenger door and the tailgate – yet again, nothing! It was only when I glanced inside the vehicle and realised the contents weren't mine that it dawned on me - neither was the car!

But what has all this got to do with trout fishing? Well, as in the latter example, I too had responded to triggers. The car was the right model and colour, and was roughly where I expected to see it. The wrong registration. The wrong contents. The detail didn't matter. The triggers got me – hooked me, if you will - and so it is with trout fishing. Show the fish a fly with the right triggers, combine that with good presentation and you are 99% there!

So, what does all this mean? Does it confirm that trout often display the same behaviours and levels of intellect as seemingly "educated" fishermen? Or does it prove that some fishermen display behaviour little different from that of a fish whose brain is the size of a pea? I know what *I* like to believe and, strangely, Mrs. Murgatroyd - who normally has no interest in or understanding of piscatorial matters - seems to think that she also has the answer!

Now, where are those Pringles…?!

The "Wright" Angle

An interview with TV's Matthew Wright

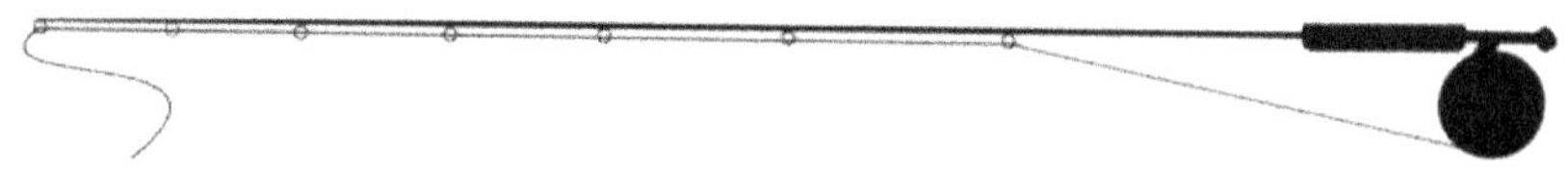

Matthew was the presenter of the now-defunct Channel 5 TV show *"The Wright Stuff"*. It was broadcast every weekday, in which Mr. Wright - along with an ever-changing panel of celebrity guests - would discuss and debate the topical issues of the week, interacting with members of the studio audience as well members of the general public via a television phone-in. The show would air live and was a huge commitment; requiring early-morning starts and a good breadth of knowledge covering a wide range of subjects. Having held such demanding media-related posts, it is little wonder that when it comes to relaxation and ways to unwind, Matthew loves to fly-fish!

We are sharing a drink in a London club frequented by people in the Arts and Media. Steven Berkoff - the celebrated writer and actor - is at a nearby table, and I have to admit to being more than a little distracted. Having recently watched film director Stanley Kubrick's interpretation of Anthony Burgess' dystopian tale *"A Clockwork Orange"* with my son Nick (one of his all-time favourite films!) in which Berkoff plays a policeman, it feels slightly surreal to now be sharing the same room as someone with such a pedigree. As soon as Matthew starts to speak about his love of (and passion for) fly fishing, however; all the disturbing, nightmarish images that the film portrays are banished, and thankfully I am back in the present. It is obvious that fishing plays a massive part in Matthew's life - and his enthusiasm is clearly evident as he guides me through his angling journey…

When Matthew was around eight years old, his father hired a boat for a family holiday on the Norfolk Broads, treating his son to a child's fishing rod at the same time. Matthew's first fish was an eel, and over the course of the two-week holiday, Matthew caught fourteen fish in total and was hooked for life! The rest, as they say, is history.

Growing up in Croydon, Matthew's early excursions were to a local coarse fishing lake with totally unsuitable tackle borrowed from his Dad, himself an occasional angler. Little did Matthew realise that much of his early lack of success could be attributed to the fact that the tackle he had borrowed was actually for sea fishing!

Ever since these early forays into the sport, Matthew has fished – starting off as a coarse fisherman in pursuit of Tench and Carp; adopting a very simple approach, and honing his watercraft skills. I asked Matthew how he became a fly fisherman, and he said that it was really by chance…

"I had often read the fly fishing pages in *'Angling Times'*, and the impression I got was that it was really only for 'toffs'," says Matthew. "Also, the terminology and tackle seemed totally incomprehensible! However - at the time, I was working as a journalist for the Daily Mirror, and I had handed in my notice. As a leaving present, the staff gave me a voucher from Farlows - and as they didn't stock much in the way of carp tackle, I took the plunge and bought a fly-fishing outfit. This coincided with a move from London to Norfolk, where I practised casting in my new back garden until I could just about get a line out. On my first outing to Narborough Lakes, I hooked a rainbow first cast, and have only ever used a fly rod since."

Today, Matthew is deeply passionate about his fishing and is a member of a couple of old established clubs that have both adopted a particularly pro-wild fish policy. In addition, he makes regular trips to Wales and the West Country - not only in search of wild trout, but also the occasional seatrout. He adds that he is rapidly developing the view that life is too short for Salmon fishing trips, given the number of variables that exist that are beyond his control…

In the past, Matthew has tried to fish a couple of times a week but has recently found this increasingly difficult to achieve. It is clear, however, from speaking with Matthew that his passion for protecting the environment, and wild fish in particular, burns particularly bright. Recently, The Wild Trout Trust appointed him a Vice President - a position that he feels very honoured to hold and takes very seriously. I asked him how this came about, and he explained: "I decided one year to have a bid on the Trusts' annual auction, and was lucky to win a days' fishing with Jon Beer" (Matthew's favourite angling writer and the current President of the Trust). "A strong friendship developed from this trip and, because of my experience in the media and PR worlds, I was delighted to accept the Trusts' offer to become a Vice President of the organisation."

I asked Matthew about fly-tying, to which he responded; "Yes, I tie my own flies but normally only when I have the time - which is very rare - and there's nothing in the house to drink! I'm quite good about tying bonefish flies. I rarely lose them, so all the effort seems to be worth it but, sometimes, busting a gut at the tying bench only to lose your precious creations on tree branches that you can't reach is like the trial of Sisyphus methinks. That said, I'm fascinated by the use of non-traditional materials: insulation from a three-core electric cable, dubbing from tumble drier lint (we've got brown towels, so it goes a nice colour!). It's amazing what you can recycle into flies."

Matthew's love of fly-fishing has taken him all over the world, including New Zealand, South Africa and a recent trip to the Himalayas, where he combined fly-fishing with another of his hobbies - motorcycling!

Saltwater fly fishing plays an increasingly large part in Matthew's fishing life and started with a trip to Cuba. However, discouraged by the considerable expense that can be incurred pursuing this, Matthew has increasingly adopted a more 'do-it-yourself' approach, exploring other regions in the Caribbean. This has now resulted in him discovering his own 'hotspots'. He has even bought a house in the region and says that "when TV has had enough of me or vice versa, I dream of operating a sustainable guiding service that benefits the local economy and respects the quarry."

Matthew's wife, Amelia, has become a particularly keen and proficient angler with an impressive tally of good-sized fish to her credit - something which gives Matthew a great sense of pride. This pride is particularly evident when he shows me photographs of her catches, both at home and abroad, freshwater and salt.

Closer to home, Matthew still loves to fish for wild trout, and although he belongs to some very august clubs, he gets just as much pleasure from fishing wild rain-fed streams in the U.K. via the various Passport schemes that now exist in numerous regions. With his cane rod and a simplified approach, I suspect that he has found the perfect antidote to the world in which he earns his living!

The Wild Trout Trust needs your support, and I know that Matthew is determined to do all he can to raise the profile of the organisation in order to protect and promote the welfare of a species that we all love. He believes that we must all do everything in our power to avoid a dystopian *Clockwork Orange*-esque future in which clean streams and wild trout are just a distant memory…

For further details on The Wild Trout Trust and its work, visit:
www.wildtrout.org

The Accidental Naturalist

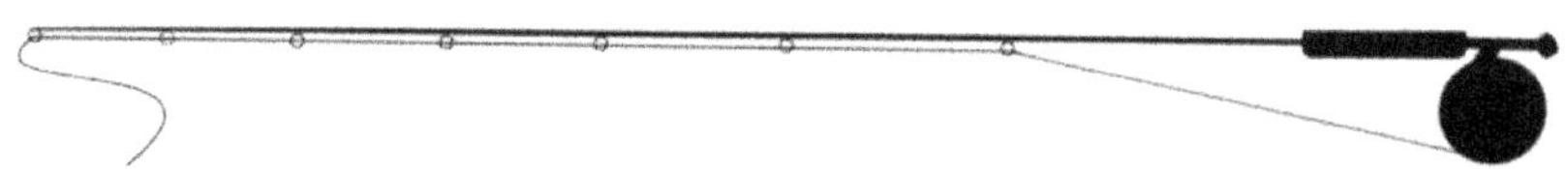

E ven the best of us will - from time to time - have a day when, whatever we do, we fail to connect with a fish. Sometimes, we seem unable to solve that eternal mystery of what the fish *want*, even though the surface of the water is covered in rises. Other times, the river just seems to be fishless; whatever we try being greeted with a resounding indifference… a blank day.

But just because the fish aren't cooperating, doesn't necessarily mean the day is a failure. One of the most magical experiences I had on the river last season involved a *complete lack of fish*!

The sun was high, the river low - fairly typical conditions. I had run the gamut of tactics from leaded nymph to dry fly - all to no avail. I had wearily worked my way back up to the bridge and was just having a few `last casts' when I suddenly had the feeling I was being watched. I froze, concentrating on the periphery of my vision. Suddenly, there it was! In broad daylight I saw a young badger at the bank, drinking from the river's cool waters. In the very same instant of my noticing the animal, it apparently became aware of *me*. For a few seconds we made eye contact until, imperceptibly, it began a subtle retreat into the leafy undergrowth. A blank day had just become a most memorable one!

Most river valleys are rich in wildlife, so we needn't have a 'blank day' if we just utilise our senses to *appreciate what is all around us*. Let's be honest; we all know if the fishing is slow, the best tactic to successfully tempt a fish is to simply cast your fly and immediately go into mental cruise control, promptly gazing off into the middle distance. Or to squint to the skies;

buzzards lazily riding the thermals high above the valley. Fish seem to sense when you're distracted, often picking that exact moment to take your fly. Of course, you won't hook the fish - but at least by appreciating all that nature has to offer, those fishless days will no longer seem *completely* blank...

Sometimes what we glimpse is so fleeting that we often wonder whether we really even saw it at all. A figment of imagination? Or wishful thinking, maybe, in much the same way we convince ourselves that a swaying frond of weed is, in fact, a large, hungry trout? At other times, however, that electric blue flash *does* return - materializing into a kingfisher! Or perhaps that chromium sub-surface glint *does* turn out to be a trout chasing shrimp. Just because we don't actually *catch* a fish, does not mean the day *must* be a failure. By taking in our surroundings, by being 'aware' (and indeed, self-aware), each day spent by the water has so much more to offer than just fish!

If you look at the illustrations in one of John Gierach's early books, *Fly Fishing Small Steams*, there is a drawing of a fishing vest showing some of the contents of its pockets. One standout item (which, I would wager, is absent from most fisherman's 'essentials'), is a pair of binoculars. Yes, I realise we all have a tendency to carry too much gear -- but if you *do* have a good quality pair of compact binoculars to hand, you will be amazed at just how much more you will enjoy and appreciate life going on around you. Handily, they can also be used to spot fish and to identify hatching insects; thereby possibly avoiding that dreaded fishless day.

Studying nature is also an excellent way of learning - and developing - your watercraft. You will learn a great deal about economy of movement, stealth and choosing your moment by watching birds and mammals as they stalk their prey. You may even discover that, if you observe the close season (as I prefer to), you actually begin to *look forward* to winter excursions! Binoculars and telescope at hand, in pursuit of warm-blooded creatures, you will likely derive just as much pleasure as you would in pursuit of trout during the warmer months!

If you fish for long enough, you cannot help but become an "*Accidental Naturalist.*" It is impossible to fish with even a small amount of success without absorbing the elements of the natural world. This enables you to approach each fishing trip with a little more anticipation, a little more *confidence*; which will ultimately result in a wholly satisfying outing - even if the results, fish-wise, may suggest otherwise…

Me, Myself & I

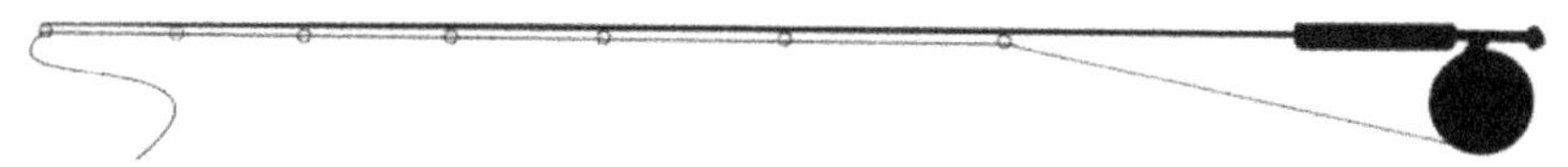

I am a solitary fisherman at heart. Well, at least I *think* I am... Perhaps it is something to do with the slightly romantic vision I have of fly fishing, no doubt fuelled by my love of North American writers who recount tales of disappearing into the wilderness for days on end. Man against nature, that sort of thing. Not that easy to replicate in the U.K. - - too many people, too little space - - but at least I can daydream. My predilection for solo fishing may, however, have more to do with my childhood...

As an only child, I naturally spent a lot of time alone and came to enjoy my own company and, by necessity, made a lot of my own entertainment. I think this is what first attracted me to fishing. I regarded it as a mainly solitary pursuit, best enjoyed in isolation. It is, by its very nature, a contemplative activity and it's much easier to sit and reflect when by yourself than when with others. I am not a particularly competitive person, and found that when fishing with friends - especially as a child - inevitably a competitive element would insidiously creep into proceedings; who caught the first? The most? The biggest?... I was (and still am) content to catch just one fish, then either stop fishing for the day or just potter about the waterside, nature-watching and enjoying the experience of being "free." I do realise that I have the privilege of living with a river at the bottom of my garden, thus allowing me to take a much more relaxed approach to my time by the water than I might otherwise do if I had to travel a distance. That's not to say I am happy to blank; I can at least admit that I do enjoy the outing more once that first fish is in the net... you know what I mean. Perhaps I *am* more competitive than I think?!

But when I reflect on my fishing life, I realise many of my most replayed memories are *not* self-centered; indeed, many of them would cease to exist had I not benefitted from the kindness, enthusiasm and generosity of others…

I remember being shown the rudiments of casting at the age of eleven or twelve by the local newsagent-come-tackle seller who, almost to order, hooked a trout and then handed me the rod to play and land the fish. He later got me into the local club. His kindness and generosity have had more of an impact on my life than he could ever have imagined. Although I regard myself as solitary, I have always belonged to clubs - even becoming the secretary of one! - and as a result I have met and fished with like-minded people who have become true friends. There have been plenty of adventures in pursuit of all sorts of fish!

Great memories such as a camping and fishing trip to The Isle of Man, fishing off the rocks for huge Pollack. We camped by the side of a disused, flooded quarry where, in the evening, we would lie on our stomachs looking down into the water to watch enormous eels rise up from the bottom and take insects off the surface. How we dreamt of pioneering dry fly fishing for eels. Unfortunately, they were, from a casting point of view, inaccessible.

There have been trips to Ireland in pursuit of Bass, Mullet and Pollack; sublime days spent wandering the surf beaches of Kerry with just a fly rod and big dreams. Big dreams inspired around the campfire the previous night, possibly fuelled by alcohol, definitely fuelled by the enthusiasm of good friends who, with their knowledge and a genuine desire of wanting you to succeed, shared their experiences and shared their secrets. I learnt more about saltwater fly fishing from them in a week than I could have done in a lifetime of fishing alone.

There have also been trips to more remote areas: the hidden Llyns of North Wales, magical Tarns up in The Lake District, weekends up to the mighty and sometimes brutal Cow Green, with more trips yet to come.

Then there is the more organised, social side of fishing. Take, for example, The Game Fair. Perhaps no longer as fishing-orientated as it used to be, but once upon a time it was an important gathering place for anglers of all types, perhaps nowadays usurped by the fantastic British Fly Fair International. In addition, there are now local branches of the Fly Dressers' Guild, and you really should do yourself a favour and go along. Not only will your fly-tying technique improve, you will glean lots of information on local fishing, and possibly make new friends!

Now that I come to think of it, I probably fish with friends a lot more often than I realised. Only last week, I had a day as a guest on one of the very best trout rivers in the country, and as long as I didn't show myself up (hopefully I didn't!), more visits will be planned in the future.

I do still love to fish alone, but realise now that if not for the kindness of many of the people I've met through my pursuit of fish, I wouldn't be half the fisherman I hope I am today! But even when fishing alone, I *am* often in the company of some of my oldest and most important companions. One in particular is my old Hardy Jet glass fibre fly rod. It has accompanied me on some of my most memorable adventures. It was a present from my parents in 1969, and I think they recognised even then how important fishing was to become in my life. Fortunately, they had the foresight and generosity to buy me the best they could afford. I have other good companions; a gorgeous Edward Barder split cane seven-and-a-half-footer, as well as a unique Marcus Warwick opal grey, carbon eight foot four weight, made for Ari Hart.

As fantastic as these are, and as privileged as I know I am to have them, if these were my *only* companions at the waterside, I know my fishing would be much the poorer for it.

Ceiriog Thoughts

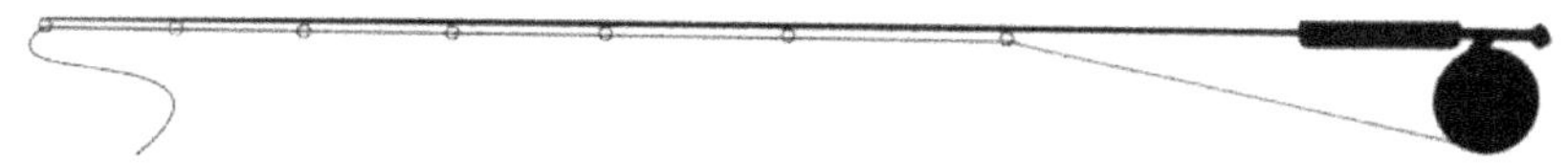

High in the Berwyn mountains, the sparkling Ceiriog springs to life and begins its tumultuous race to the sea via the Dee. Reputably the fastest flowing river in Wales, the Ceiriog runs roughly west to east. By the time it reaches the bottom of my garden - approximately halfway through its journey - it has matured into a delightful small stream; in most places no more than fifteen to twenty feet across, but still bright and sparkling as it forges its way down the valley.

The Ceiriog Valley (known locally as the 'Valley of the Poets'), is home to many writers and artists who take inspiration from the area's lush landscape and rich mixture of history and myth. From my back door, I often watch and listen as the frothing braid of currents pushes past the ancient battleground of Crogen, where the invading English were defeated by the defending Welsh. The battleground is flanked by the river on one side, and by the *'Gate of the Dead'* on the other - an area set in ancient woodland featuring thousand-year-old oaks that reach skywards towards the dominating castle above. The river then tumbles below a steeply wooded bank featuring deep, foreboding caves - home to... well, who knows what?

On this border river, it's possible to hook your trout in England and land it in Wales - having taken just a couple of steps during the playing. The wild trout are like quicksilver, and whether your choice of weapon is Tenkara or Tonkin, graphite or glass – the fish respond well to most methods of fly fishing, as long as you are stealthy in your approach. And this approach will pay dividends in other ways; the valley is rich in wildlife, and the river attracts creatures of every kind to its banks. Only last season, I stood transfixed as a young badger, in broad daylight, came down to drink from the cool waters.

Buzzards, Sparrowhawks, Dippers, Kingfishers… all are commonplace, along with numerous other birds, mammals and insects in sufficient numbers to turn every visit to the river into a magical experience.

A wild trout out of this wild river is as good as fishing gets!

Trance Casting

Thankfully, in the eyes of most liberal-minded people, the carrying of a fly rod can validate a number of activities that might otherwise have resulted in an unpleasant confrontation or, at the very least, in the police being called. I'm not talking about the blatant childish joy of wading in rivers or climbing up trees in order to spot fish. I'm not even talking about wandering around the countryside in the early hours when chasing sea trout. No. What I'm talking about is how the insidious nature of fly fishing can, if allowed, influence almost every aspect of your life. In extreme cases, it can present as a Zen-like state that, in the wrong circumstances, can cause problems for all concerned.

Let me elaborate. My own approach to fly fishing has, in some quarters, come to be regarded as slightly eccentric. With the passing of each year, the earth seems to spin at an ever-increasing rate. I have therefore made a conscious decision to slow down my approach to most things, particularly with regard to my fishing. I know there is an oft-quoted piscatorial doctrine which preaches that if your fly isn't in the water then you won't catch any fish, but this is only true up to a point. Since slowing down, I'm finding that in certain circumstances my success rate has improved. Less really is more!

In the past when I arrived at the water, I was anxious not to waste any precious time and would tackle up as quickly as possible and start fishing. Ironically, in my haste not to waste time, I was, in fact, doing just that! I would make straight for familiar fishing spots, tie on a pattern of fly that had worked previously and fish. Usually, I was wasting my time. To all intents and purposes, I was fishing on 'auto-pilot', and the results were disappointing to say the least. My approach to the water was not as careful as it should have been, and often I would walk right up to the water's edge (or even wade in as deep as I could) before casting towards the horizon. Any trout were long gone before I even started to fish!

It was longer than I care to admit before the penny dropped. The key to my approach now is movement - or rather the lack of it. My wife might just comment that keeping movement to a minimum has long been a cornerstone of my approach to life in general - not just my fishing. Sometimes I think she doesn't understand me.

However, lack of movement is *definitely* an advantage when trying to get close to a wild creature - and especially so when fly fishing which, by its very nature, involves a lot of arm-waving, guaranteed to betray your existence to the very fish you are trying to catch. So my doctrine is now based on stealth - and it seems to work. The other good news is that if like me, you are a fairly indifferent caster, it doesn't matter - you will still catch lots of fish, sometimes by casting hardly at all! The key to all this is: on arrival at the water - don't fish. Observe, listen, and be as still as you can - think Heron. As you sit quietly, just watching and waiting, you will be amazed at the wildlife – including the trout - that will, after a relatively short time, reveal their presence to you. Watch the margins. I promise you will often see trout in just a few inches of water - the very same water that previously, in your haste, you would have waded through or cast over. If you do nothing else, keep below the horizon, reduce your false casting and don't wade unless circumstances dictate that you must.

Alas, as I alluded to, there is a downside to this approach. In adapting my modus operandi, I have slowly become aware that my behaviour may, to some, appear slightly odd and at times just plain *weird:* I had crept on all fours into position behind a bush, hoping to conceal my presence from any fish lying in what appeared to be a perfect pool - all I needed was for the fish to reveal itself, as I knew it surely would. I watched and waited... and waited... and waited.

After a while, I sank into a trance-like state. The world closed in around me. All that existed was me and the ever-decreasing area of river on which I had become transfixed. I began to hallucinate, seeing huge trout undulating just below the surface before they morphed back into just waving strands of weed. Suddenly, there was the real thing! In slow motion, I reached for my rod. At that moment my dream-like reverie was shattered by a loud and aggressive *"Oi!"*, bellowed from just behind my left ear. I nearly jumped out of my skin and into the river. I shot to my feet, only to be confronted by a particularly large and robust character who demanded to know why I had apparently been staring, from behind a bush, into his mother's bedroom window for the last half hour. It slowly dawned on me that, to anyone living in the large bungalow on the opposite bank, my actions may have appeared open to question. Having assured my aggressor that I was only looking for fish, his attitude seemed to mellow into a bemused indifference, more usually reserved for those with too little to do and too much time in which to do it.

Now whenever I fish that particular pool, I feel compelled to make it obvious that I'm just an innocent fly fisherman. I walk straight up to the bank, into the water, and start casting. My old approach. Of course, I never catch anything…

Back to the Future

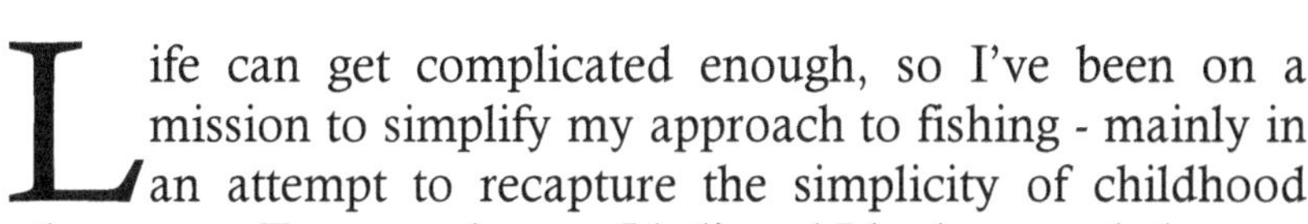

Life can get complicated enough, so I've been on a mission to simplify my approach to fishing - mainly in an attempt to recapture the simplicity of childhood adventures. To some degree, I believed I had succeeded …

In recent years, I've done most of my fishing with split cane rods, a simple reel, floating line and a few essential bits and pieces of tackle carried in my pockets. Generally, this approach has worked well. I don't think I've caught fewer fish, and I've certainly enjoyed my fishing and felt content with my choice of tackle. The other great benefit is, I've convinced myself I've saved money. Somebody once said that the secret to achieving happiness in this increasingly consumer-orientated society is through contentment. Wanting what you've got - not getting what you think you want. By adopting my simplified approach, effectively turning my back on all the latest tackle developments, I've been able (to a significant degree) to live a fishing life that's been pretty much oblivious to the latest proclamations of the tackle industry's marketing men. Until, that is, I heard the *'T' word*.

I know some will think I'm already living in the past by embracing bamboo rods and eschewing chest waders, but that's nothing compared to what has happened to me over the last few weeks. If I were to admit to you that the rod I've been using recently has more in common with the stuff Walton and Cotton fished with, then you could be forgiven for thinking I had finally 'lost it'. But in actual fact, what I've 'lost' in my search for the simple life *is the reel*.

And Tenkara is what I've 'found'. Not to get into talk of reinventing the wheel, but this is another example of there being nothing new under the sun. History really does repeat itself - even in the sleepy backwaters of the angling world!

Tenkara is a traditional Japanese method of fishing the small mountain streams of that country, utilising very simple tackle. Typically a long telescopic rod of approximately eleven-to-thirteen feet in length, with a line of about one-and-a-half times the rod's length, comprising a furled leader or level length of line, a tippet and a fly. The line is attached directly to the tip of the rod - no reel! How simple can life get? Of course, I had to have a go! The irony in all this, of course, is that I was once again falling victim to the very people I was trying so hard to avoid! The marketing men were reeling me in. Or perhaps not... I sought consolation by telling myself that at least I wasn't buying another reel. Thus, suitably equipped, I ventured out onto the Nidd.

My first trip (although fruitless; *fish*-less, as it were!), did teach me a few lessons. I fished using the furled leader, which was fine when fishing nymphs or wet flies where 'turnover' isn't as critical, but as soon as I changed to a dry fly, presentation became terrible. On my second trip, in similar conditions, things improved significantly. I replaced the furled leader with one of level fluorocarbon. This turned the fly over in the breeze with little difficulty. A great advantage of Tenkara is that, by collapsing my rod, I'm able to access overgrown parts of the river that previously I would have bypassed. After hooking and landing three fish ranging from six-to-twelve inches, I felt I was starting to get a real feel for the style. I couldn't help thinking of my collection of reels at home; the money I'd spent on them and what I might end up doing with them. If history teaches us anything at all about the human condition, it is this: *we're never content*. Inevitably, some people have *already* started trying to overcomplicate Tenkara! How long will it be before somebody designs a contraption to store line and allow larger fish to run? Perhaps I'd better hold on to those reels back home a little longer after all...!

The past, however, couldn't help with a solution to the biggest problem I encountered when fishing the Tenkara method: what to do with my 'spare' hand. Essentially, Tenkara is a one-handed style of fishing - because there is no reel or line to shoot or retrieve, the hand not holding the rod is redundant for much of the time. In the end, I opted for holding a wading staff. I did try putting my hand in my pocket, but that just felt too casual - I at least like to *look* as though I'm making an effort!

Some exponents suggest placing your free hand on your hip when fishing… but I fear that could generate unkind rumours from some of the… *less charitable*… club members.
Something along the lines of not being a *"reel man!"*

The Armchair Angler

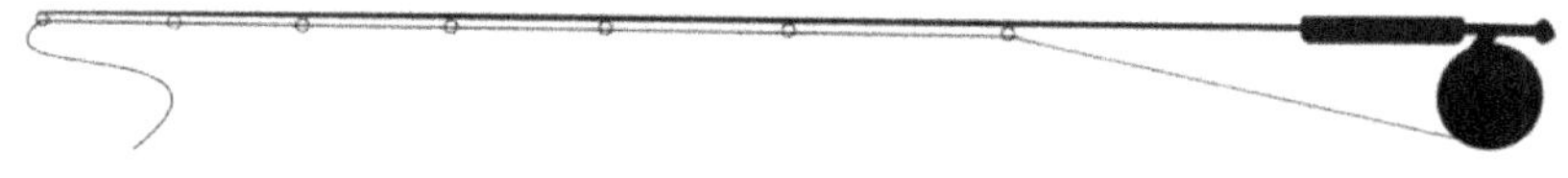

This fly fishing lark isn't all it's cracked up to be. No matter how many books I read on the subject, I never seem to improve. Relaxing, contemplative, good for the soul... I don't think so. In my experience it's stressful, frustrating and expensive. As for being good for the soul, I can't remember the number of times I've been prepared to sell mine to Beelzebub in return for just *one* slightly-larger-than-average fish. And to make matters worse, even the Devil himself wasn't interested in doing a deal with me! Talk about suffering from low self-esteem. All in the name of trying to outwit a fish.

Think back to your most recent trips to the waterside. If your experiences are anything like mine, they could well be neatly summarised under the heading:

Location, location, location.

No, not the estate agent's favourite mantra – rather, the description of a typical recent fishing expedition. Now, you may think that sounds nice and neat and tidy, but come along with me and I will show you the reality!

Firstly, *location*. I don't mean where to fish - that agony will come later. I mean, *where is the spare spool for my reel?* I'm sure it was in the cupboard with the other spare spools for my numerous other reels! You may be asking yourself why I don't use one of those, seeing as I have so many other reels to choose from. But what you don't realise is that the reel in question is my *lucky* reel, and to not use it would surely spell disaster! An hour of searching later, I discover it in a dark corner in the boot of the car. Tackle now gathered, I'm ready to go. Not *too* badly delayed, all things considered.

The next problem is, of course, *actual* location...

Because of the reel incident, I'm running later than planned; the small still water I'd wanted to visit may well be occupied by other anglers by now. It really won't stand too many at any one time. Still, I decide to give it a go…

Thanks to a road closure, a lengthy detour and a particularly slow tractor, I arrive – as suspected - to find the lake bristling with those aforementioned anglers, all the best spots already taken. Time to put *'plan B'* into action! Location number two is the river. I will, of course, have to nip home to pick up my river tackle. If I get a move on, I could be on the river by late morning...

It's just 'noon by the time I arrive. I make my way under the bridge and down to the weir. The question is, do I go to a favourite spot: a nicely-proportioned pool with just about the right amount of cover to make casting a little tricky but also attractive to at least a couple of fish where even *I'm* capable of catching one? Or do I choose the difficult option: to start up by the bridge and work my way upstream, locating feeding fish as I go? Rather typically, I decide on the easy option and head for my favourite pool.

The half-mile trek takes me past a few good-looking places, but I stick to my plan and resist the temptation to cast a fly until I reach my intended destination. I sit for a few minutes under a young tree and study the water, looking for signs of life, eventually spotting the flash of a fish as it turns in the current. I slowly get to my knees, attaching an artificial shrimp to my leader. Too many casts to even begin to count are made and *still* the fish shows total indifference to my offerings. I find myself mentally suggesting to anyone who may be receptive to my thoughts that I may be prepared to do some sort of deferred deal involving my soul, just for one *small-ish* fish. If I were fishing in the sea, I might call it a *'Soul-for-a-Sole'* kind of deal, but since I'm not, I won't. No divine, piscine, or any other type of intervention occurs, and I decide to forsake the pool and fish my way back to the car. I catch nothing.

Back home, I wonder if the agonies of real fishing are no longer for me. Perhaps I'm losing my touch. I make myself a drink, settle in a comfortable chair and open my favourite fishing book. Within the pages of the book I can lose myself in a world of pristine rivers, perfect casts and large, hungry trout that take my elegantly self-tied flies as if they were the real thing. Within the pages of the book, disasters rarely occur and even when they do there is usually a happy ending. Armchair angling! This has got to be the way forward for a jaded fisherman like myself. Replace grief with relief and memories with dreams - even if they're virtual! But as great as armchair angling is, I know it will never fully capture that exquisite moment when the fish takes your fly. That split-second of ecstasy when you connect with a mysterious creature of such wild beauty, savage innocence and innate dignity. An experience that can only be hinted at on the page, but one that once tasted, insidiously roots itself into your being, driving you back to the waterside again and again for another fix.

So while I do love my books, they can only hint at the true pleasure of the real thing. And that, I suppose, is what keeps me returning. When I go fishing, it's not only the trout I'm trying to capture, but possibly some abstract experience. How closely one depends upon the other I'm not sure, but catching a fish is not an unimportant element. Perhaps, if I search hard enough, the answer is to be found in one of my books after all. In fact, I think I've already found the answer: it's in *"Fisherman"* by Anthony Pearson.

You should read it. I'm going to.

Again.

The Boomerang Trout

Angling: the contemplative man's recreation. Well, it is if you're not catching any fish! This past season, I've had a lot of time to contemplate. Time to consider life, death, the universe and - more importantly - how unfair it all can be.

It was a warm, sunny day in May. Nothing was stirring down at the lake - no breeze and no sign of fish. I reeled in, stowed the rod, laid back and daydreamed as the boat drifted gently towards the far bank. On this occasion, my main contemplative subject was my love of fishing. Specifically, fishing with cane rods - and how I might convince my wife that my present collection of just four is not in the slightest way excessive! That it demonstrates, in fact, great *restraint* on my part to the extent that, on this trip, I had been "forced" to fish with a carbon "stick", due to a gap in my bamboo armoury...

Of course, while I *do* have a strong affinity for fishing with cane, I would never admit to her that there *are* times when cane is not always the best tool for the job. In much the same way the most beautiful women do not necessarily make the best wives (the present Mrs. Murgatroyd excepted!), or an Aston Martin is not always the best vehicle for every journey. A delicate and beautiful cane wand, however great it feels and however attractive it may look, is not necessarily the ablest companion when the going gets tough.

But I digress...

My contemplative doze had been interrupted by the boat gently grounding in the extensive weed beds in the shallow water on the western bank. I unshipped the oars and carefully maneuvered the boat out into deeper water before lowering the anchor and resuming fishing. After several fruitless casts with a damselfly nymph, I was thinking about calling it a day. Then, out of the corner of my eye, I noticed a dark shape move out from under the edge of the weed bed from which I had extracted the boat. I froze as I watched the fish nose its way around the perimeter of the weed bed. After a few minutes - and with as little movement as possible - I dropped the fly close to the fish. Instantly, the trout swung around and took the fly. I lifted the rod and felt a satisfying lunge as the fish reacted.

The fight was strange and prolonged, and I was convinced that the fish was foul hooked; it almost seemed to be coming in sideways! Eventually, the trout was at the side of the boat - a nice brownie of about a pound and a half. The fly was visible, set firmly in its scissors. The reason for the strange fight now became clear: the poor fish, due to a deformity of the spine, was almost boomerang-shaped! Despite its handicap, the fish (although a little on the thin side for its length) seemed to be in good health. I carefully unhooked the trout in the water and watched it swim away, none the worse for its adventure.

Having now had this small success, I decided to have a few more casts before packing up. After twenty minutes or so, I spotted a fish close to where the "boomerang trout" had been. Again, I gently cast the damselfly nymph towards the fish. And once again, the fish turned without hesitation and took the fly. This time, upon feeling the hook, the fish went straight into the weed bed and all went solid. After what seemed an age of giving the fish slack line and then exerting pressure from different angles, a large clump of weed gradually came away with the fish well and truly buried in its midst. Eventually, I managed to get the fish - and the weed! - into the landing net, heaving it on board.

As I slowly recovered the fish from the weed, I couldn't believe my eyes. This was the "boomerang trout!" It had lived up to its name and come back!

Now, this wasn't the first time I'd caught the same fish twice. Previously, I had caught a grayling from the River Nidd on the same fly. This was in the same location on consecutive days (the fish being identifiable by a scar on its left flank), but to catch such an unusual fish twice in such a short space of time really did give me something to contemplate…

As I rowed back to the boathouse, the incident set me thinking about how unfair life can be; not only for humans - and anglers in particular - but sometimes for our quarry as well.

Later that evening, as I discussed the day's strange events with my wife, I told her that I felt life and fate had played a cruel trick on the boomerang trout. She pointed out to me that it was not as cruel as the trick that life had played on us as a couple. Because in the space of just 20-odd years, we had gone from being compared to Barbie and Ken to *Deirdre and Ken*!

Contemplate *that*!

Revenge of the Killer Fish

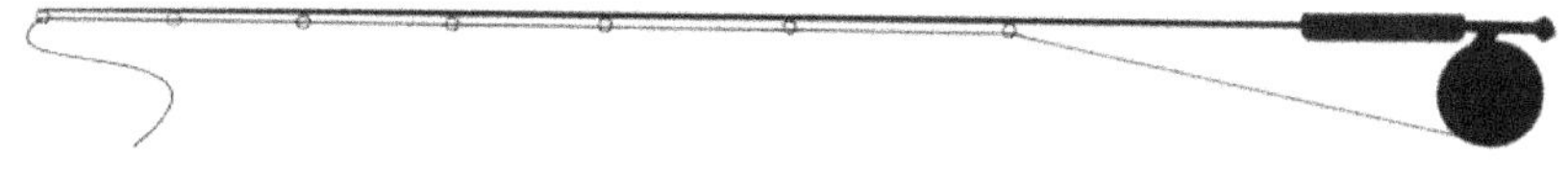

There are no *actual* killer fish in the tale of woe that follows. In fact, there are hardly any fish at all. As usual, it is probably all in my mind. I, however, prefer to think of the following series of mishaps as revenge on the part of the fish - after all, if it isn't piscine retaliation, then it could only be total incompetence on my part. I'm certain that anybody who knows me well will confirm that that is unlikely...

I was around twelve years old, and the proud owner of a Hardy fly rod - my first rod *not* bought with Green Shield stamps – rather, a present from my parents. I always cycled to the river and usually fastened the rod to the crossbar of my bike. On this particular occasion, I was in a hurry, and decided to ride with one hand holding the rod, the other on the handlebars. What could possibly go wrong? Well, only one thing *did* go wrong; the need to control the bike! It was too late when I realised that I needed to use my 'rod' hand to operate the rear brake and, as I careered out of control and around the bend, I grabbed at the brake lever, at the same time deftly inserting the rod into the spokes of the rapidly spinning front wheel. That was when my two-piece rod became a four-piece, and I went head-over-heels over the handlebars.

One-nil to the fish, or was it an own goal?

Fast-forward a couple of years... I was sitting in the stern of the boat. Ken was on the jetty, and passed the "Seagull" outboard motor down to me, ready for me to clamp on to the transom. At least, he *thought* he had passed the motor to me. Whether he let go too soon or I tried to take hold too late is still the subject of heated debate. Whatever the truth, the outcome was the same; the motor clearly visible eight feet down, lying on the bottom. (Incidentally -- when eventually retrieved, the motor started first time!)

Two-nil to the fish, or was it an own goal?

Over the years, other unfortunate events occurred. Our tent, for example, was trampled by crazed cows while we were away attempting to catch fish. Who knew fish and cows could communicate?!

Once, while fishing a high mountain lake on a bitterly cold day early in the season, I somehow managed to stick the hook, well past the barb, into my finger. It was only due to the freezing temperature that I was able to rip the hook from my flesh without too much pain. I left my blood on the fly in the hope that it might attract a fish. It didn't.

As I grew older and more experienced, I gained confidence and started to catch a few more fish. I read the fishing press avidly, and over the years developed a liking for 'catch and release' - only taking fish for the pot when I really needed them. Now, you would think that this might have won me some favour with my quarry…

My role models were people like the two Brians - Harris and Clarke, Neil Patterson, the great Steve Parton, and of course John Goddard. Mr. Goddard advocates a method of releasing fish in the water by utilising the tip of the rod and essentially using the tip ring as a disgorger, thus eliminating the need to handle the fish. I, where appropriate, have adopted this method. By this time, I had also developed a penchant for excruciatingly expensive cane fly rods. The fish knew this. I hooked a small trout; no more than eight inches. I brought it into the bank and proceeded to use the Goddard method of unhooking. The trout did a very small backflip at the critical moment and inflicted a huge break in the rod - four inches from the tip ring. Through a red mist of disbelief and tears, I gently unhooked the spiteful little fish, watched him swim gleefully away, and went home to telephone Mr. Barder, the rod-maker.

Yes, I have caught a few fish on and off over the years - but I can't help believing that they have had more fun out of me than I have out of them. And the misfortune continues to this day. A salmon fishing trip, for instance - lots of money spent, and everything planned down to the last detail. The first day on the water - no fish. I was climbing out of the river when I stumbled up the bank. The sole had come off my wading boot. I didn't have a spare pair and neither did anybody else in the party. To try to fish without the sole would have ruined a very expensive pair of waders. I spent the next twelve hours sitting in front of a roaring fire on what was the hottest night of the year, trying to dry out the felt sole and boot so that I could superglue them together and carry on fishing the next day. I missed breakfast but, bleary-eyed and shattered, I managed to fish the next day after all. I didn't catch anything that day, the next day or the next day after that! Then, it was time to go home. Oh, how those fish must have laughed!

More recently, I was invited to fish a very exclusive trout stream. I had all my best gear and tried hard to look as if I knew what I was doing. I assembled my rod and started to attach my prized reel. I began to tighten the reel seat and discovered - to my dismay - that instead of making the real secure, the more I turned the threaded ring on the reel seat, I was forcing the butt of the rod away from the handle.

I watched helplessly as my treasured reel fell off the rod and, as if in slow-motion, directly onto a conveniently placed rock (those evil trout, up to their old tricks again!!), with just enough force to buckle the spool and render the reel unusable. As fate would have it, I didn't have a spare reel with me. Which, of course, every trout in the river must have known. This was just another part of their fiendish plan. Conspiracy theory or not, it must be true. Otherwise, this latest event in a long line of mishaps could only be explained as total incompetence on my part...!

Mind Games

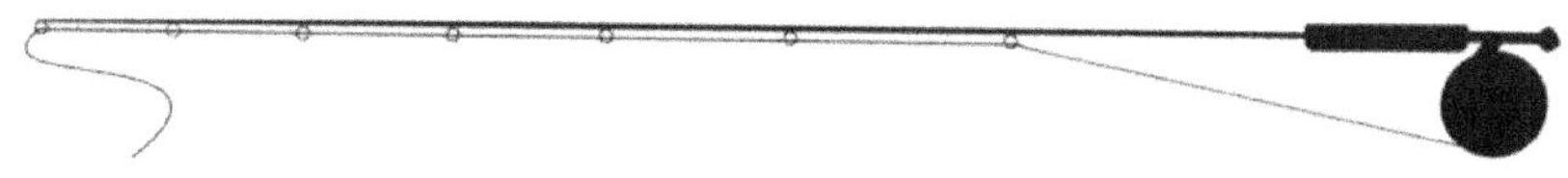

I must have been thirteen; maybe fourteen…

Dusk slowly smothered the pool, sucking out its last breaths into a silent mist that cloaked and choked us in wary anticipation. Every covert movement, every sound; amplified, intrusive.

The river and the night quickly wore us down with a relentless campaign of whispers and half-heard words. Anxious and nervous, we blindly stumbled along its greasy flanks.

Earlier in the day, we had each selected our spots - a comfortable perch, enough room to cast and easy access to the water for landing fish.

Now, in the darkness, all seemed lost - washed away by the dark, brooding river. We fished where we could, casting our lines into the unknown - frail connectors to another world - telegraphing back strange vibrations of misinformation.

When it hit, the sound was like that of a small car dropping from a great height into the river. Even before the monsoon of freezing water had finished raining down on us, we fled - grasping at each other in the darkness for reassurance and direction. We didn't stop until we made the relative comfort of the nearest street-lamp.

Later on, denying the truth, we convinced ourselves and others that a gang of poachers had thrown a rock into the water. They must have been trying to frighten us off so they could re-set the illegal night lines that we often discovered when fishing that particular stretch.

Now - older, wiser and realising that fear often plays a bigger part in life than we would care to admit, I can at last face up to the facts. This was the night that the fish turned the tables.

What we had heard that night was the sound of a huge sea trout leaping in the darkness. Our intended quarry had, in one well-timed jump, defeated us with both power and grace, in a subliminal mind game we could never win…

Even now, thirty-odd years later, night fishing *still* makes me nervous!

A Touch of Glass

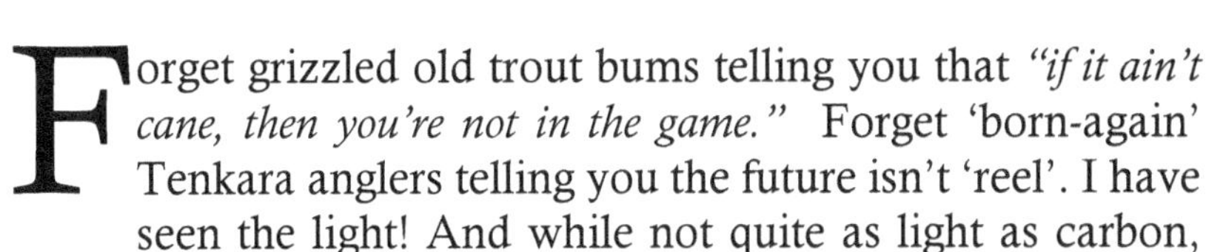

Forget grizzled old trout bums telling you that *"if it ain't cane, then you're not in the game."* Forget 'born-again' Tenkara anglers telling you the future isn't 'reel'. I have seen the light! And while not quite as light as carbon, it's light enough for me. What I'm talking about is *glass*. Yes, fibreglass. The *only* choice for a child of the sixties.

Think about it. If you're about my age you'll probably recall that when you were a kid, cane rods seemed particularly unappealing. All the ones I came across were heavy and about as straight as an MP's expense claim. They looked like something that should be supporting your Granddad's sweet peas down on the allotment. Fibreglass, on the other hand... it was light(*ish*), it came in a range of bright colours (reflecting the psychedelic fashions of the decade!) and when you hooked a fish, it adopted a bend even more extreme than Druids at Brands Hatch. Every fish hooked just *had* to be a monster. Yes, fibreglass was the future. And more importantly, it was affordable. I had glass rods from Woolworths – complete with plastic spring-loaded reel seat and plastic sleeves securing the rod rings – and rods bought with several million Green Shield stamps! Yes, on the whole they were pretty abysmal – but no worse than the cane rods I came across at the time. And the bonus of course was that you could use your glass rod to beat your way through swathes of nettles to access unfished parts of the river and, if the fishing was slow, the tip section could be used as a sword in fencing games with your mates! No need for a lifetime guarantee. Try *that* with carbon or cane...

Over the years, I have continued to fish with one of my most-prized possessions; a glass Hardy Jet, bought for me by my parents upon realising how severe my obsession had become. For a glass rod of the late sixties, the Jet was a pretty remarkable rod. Not too floppy, good to cast with (it was named after the initials of its designer, the casting champion John E. Tarrantino) and sporting a tasteful dark-brown finish much more suited to creeping up on fish than the fluorescent green that all those other makers were using.

I don't deny that, like most others, I have been seduced over the years by carbon and the race towards finding a rod weighing less than a supermodel's eyelash – but why? We all seem to want a rod lighter than air, yet at the same time walk around in fishing waistcoats even heavier than my wife's handbag! How light does a rod have to be? I like a little weight in my fly rods, just as I do in my reels – I like to *know* I've been fishing.

Over the years glass rods all but disappeared from the mainstream, and it was rare to come across anyone but the slightly bewildered using one. As a result, once my brief fling with carbon had burned itself out, I found myself attracted to split cane. Now modern split cane rod design is just about as far removed from the rods of my youth as Chris Hoy's bike is from the Penny Farthing. Of course, I amassed a large collection of cane rods, and love them for their beauty. I also fear for their wellbeing in the same way I fear for the joy of youth. I know it can't last, and that at some point it will be lost forever – to be replaced by a bent gait, creaking joints and a flaking finish. But now, I need worry no more. Glass is back and how!

Modern glass rods are a joy to own and use and, as more and more of the mainstream manufacturers reintroduce them to their ranges, the choice is growing. But don't just consider the big tackle companies. There are many artisan rod builders out there, producing fantastic rods on a variety of American and Japanese blanks, with actions to rival the best cane, and in some cases carbon, rods. I love to use my glass rods on small intimate waters where the fishing is up close and personal, and where the ability of glass to cast a very short line beautifully, really comes into its own…

If you are too young to have become too attached to any particular type of rod, and are tired of carbon dating and think cane is a pain, do yourself a favour. Bring a little glass into your life.

Touched by Izaak

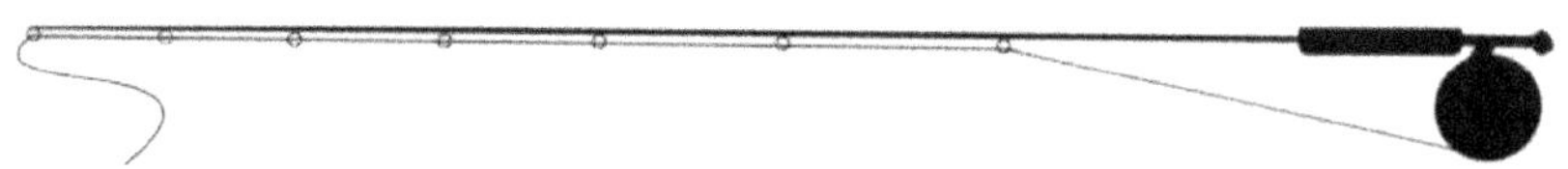

The Nidd. Deep mid-winter, snow and ice everywhere. Grayling nowhere. The water in which I've now been wading for over two hours feels colder than a landlord's heart. I can't stop myself questioning my own sanity: what madness has brought me here? I've left my son, Nick, at home reading *"Misery"*. I ponder whether Stephen King has ever fished a frozen North Yorkshire river. 'Misery' just about sums it up. (I should make it clear I'm talking *relative* misery – not the real thing. *Who said fishermen are prone to exaggeration??*) As the call of home grows stronger, my memories unravel to a day of over forty years ago - - an event I had always regarded as a blessing but which, on reflection, some might call a curse…

Pond-dipping and hunting newts in a tiny, neglected body of water, I suddenly became aware of what I perceived at the time to be a sizeable fish. For a brief moment, it remained suspended mid-water, before disappearing back into the murky depths. And although I never saw it again, it has stayed in my mind's eye ever since.

The infatuation must have come from *somewhere…* and I'm certain it was that first brief glimpse into another world; my own personal Narnia, acting as a hook, capturing me for life and making me a willing prisoner of my own addiction.

And it *is* an addiction. An obsession that, at times, can fill every waking moment and even spill over into sleep, fuelling ever more ambitious dreams which, more often than not, spiral completely out of control - firing the imagination and resulting in madcap forays in pursuit of the uncatchable. Dreams that are destined to end in failure and frustration. Dreams that may easily grow into resentment toward the minutiae of everyday life that conspire to keep you from the water - in other words, a kind of resentment towards 'reality'.

Trying to fathom the nature of this addiction is tricky. It doesn't take long, however, to realise that nature - unlike many aspects of modern life - is, if nothing else, *honest*. And although she rewards and punishes with equal indifference, it's this honesty that is, I suspect, a fundamental part of the attraction of fishing.

And that got me thinking; if *I'm* being honest, how has this addiction impacted on my life?

Is it just a coincidence that I find myself living in a town -- possibly the only town in the country -- boasting *three* dedicated fly-fishing shops? (Three shops, coincidentally, that are also dedicated to relieving me of any spare cash that might come my way!). Is it also *just* a coincidence that I find myself living in a house with a beck at the bottom of the garden, with said beck possessing a healthy stock of wild trout? I could go on…

But would I really want my life to be any different? I may not be a high-flyer or a success in the eyes of many. Unlike a number of my neighbours, I don't have a huge house or an Aston Martin. As a matter of fact, my collection of fishing tackle is probably worth *more* than my car! I think I like to kid myself that I have my priorities in order!

My bank account may be empty, but my memory bank is full. Full to capacity with unique and priceless fishy images! The earliest memories banked when I was a child, memories of long summer days learning to cast on a small Welsh river and catching eager, greedy salmon parr which I believed, in my ignorance, to be small wild trout. Long bright days spent honing my skills and feeding my dreams…

Now, as I stand in a freezing river, creeping paralysis clawing its way up my body, do I regret being touched by the spirit of Izaak at such an early age? Do I yearn for the life that might have been, had I not suffered such a distraction? Would I trade my days on the bank for a career in the bank? Definitely not! I regard my addiction as one of the best things that could have happened to me. Fly fishing is something I am meant to do, that I *have* to do. It has proven to be one of the main constants in my life, something I can return to again and again. I'm certain in the knowledge that, whatever life casts my way, I can always rely on the rivers, lakes and seas, their inhabitants and their surroundings, to replenish my soul in a way that nothing else – even an Aston Martin – ever could…

I like to think Izaak's touch has at least made me a more complete person. Becoming a more *compleat angler*, however, may take just a little more time on the water – whatever the weather!

The Name Game

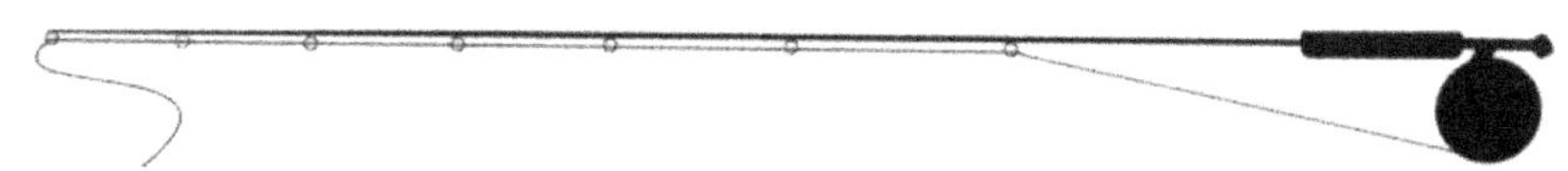

The adage *"there's more to fishing than catching fish"* is fine if you're feeling smug having caught a few - but if the net is still dry, it's just another fisherman's lie.

Where the river forks around a small shingle and scrub island, I saw Tony. He was standing mid-stream, flicking his fly under a tangle of alder bushes on the far bank. I watched the fly travel no more than eighteen inches before vanishing from sight. Tony's rod hooped over. At that moment, he spotted me. "Try a Coachman", he called. I nodded and carried on upstream.

I rounded a bend to see Ron emerging from the river, his dripping net cradling a 10-inch brownie. "Third one today!" he called. "Try a Butcher, down and across. Never fails!"

Over the next two hours, I tried a 'Butcher', then a 'Bloody Butcher' and finally, a 'Bloody Coachman'!

Despondent, I sat and let the smoke of the Kelly Kettle carry my thoughts. Suddenly, I just knew that I was going to catch fish!

Awash with inspiration, I dug out my hand vice and tied a small dark fly; borrowing some features from the Butcher, and some from the Coachman. Ego now rampant, I conjured up suitable names for my creation. I visualised articles in the fishing press toasting its success!

I ended the day with three fish and convinced myself that yes, there was indeed more to fishing than catching fish.

Later that evening, I recounted the day to my wife, Lesley, and asked her what name I should give this new fly. "You don't get it, do you?" she grinned. "Tony was a bus driver - he used a Coachman. Ron's family are butchers..."

"So, what are you saying?" I asked, a little puzzled.

"You have no choice", she said. "You must call the fly 'The Dark Deceiver' - after all, you *are* an Estate Agent!"

A Good Place

As a fly fisherman, my abilities - from a technical viewpoint and in the eyes of most of my friends - can, at best, be described only as incompetent. As a practicing incompetent, however, I believe that I am probably at the top of my game. So of course, I recognise that I should gratefully accept all the help I can get. When Nick called me to say he knows a good place, naturally my ears pricked up...

4.15am: It's dark, cold and hasn't stopped raining for over twelve hours. I stumble around the house, trying to avoid the creaking floorboards in an effort not to wake the rest of my family. I *think* I've collected all my gear, although in the half-light it's hard to be sure. I've been advised to come prepared. We're going to a really good place, but we need to get there early in order to beat the crowds. Success, apparently, depends very much on the ability to quickly switch tactics to suit the conditions. I assume, with some misgiving, that this is code for *"bring every bit of kit you possess!"*

I wait by the front door, sheltering beneath the storm porch from the freezing rain. I remind myself that this is supposed to be fun. Nick eventually arrives and, as he helps me load my gear into his Jeep, I sense he has detected in my demeanor a trace of doubt and scepticism about the whole escapade. "You're going to love this place!" he exclaims, trying to reassure me. "It's really good! But we do need to get there as early as possible" he advises, "otherwise the best spots will have been taken by the locals."

It's around a two-hour drive to the water, during which Nick tells me about his past visits to our destination. It soon becomes clear that this river holds a very special place in his heart. It has given him some outstanding memories – over thirty fish a day in some cases - as well as some memorable individual specimens. Twenty-inch-plus browns and wild rainbows, not to mention huge grayling!

As we approach the river, we pull off the main road and onto a dirt track. This leads us over a couple of cattle grids, before dropping down to a small grass enclosure beside a ramshackle timber fishing hut. To Nick's relief, there are no other vehicles. It looks as though the early start was worthwhile!

During the journey eastward the weather has gradually improved. And although there has been some rain, the river looks in fine fettle. The sun is pushing out a few weak rays and the birds are singing. This really *does* look like a good place! I'm becoming cautiously optimistic…!

Now, as I'm fishing as Nick's guest, it is only right that I should take his advice. After all, he knows the water well and wants me to have a good day. At this point I should make it clear that I am twice Nick's age and, as such, it is possible that I have become somewhat set in my ways. This is important because what follows is a good example of the 'generation gap', and how it applies to fly fishing as much as any other aspect of life.

I have my favourite rod: a split cane 7'9" two-piece built for a four-weight line, which I tend to use for most of my fishing and, as usual and without really thinking, I start to tackle up. Nick throws me a glance which I instantly recognise as questioning – challenging, even.

He looks at my rod.

"That's a really nice rod you've got there, but I think you may want something with a little more *backbone*. A little more *reach*. Something a little more *technical*…". I ponder for a moment on what a technical fishing rod may look like, when Nick answers my question by handing me an eleven-foot stick of carbon. It surely does *look* technical, but it's not very *pretty*. I think that matters. Trout are beautiful creatures, and we should honour their beauty by fishing for them with gear that has had at least *some* hours of skill and craft invested in it, rather than something that has been mass-produced for the lowest price in some far-away land…

I don't want to sound elitist or precious about this, but the 'Bakewell' fly rod built by Richard Holman is everything you would want a hand-planed cane rod to be; beautiful to look at, comfortable to hold and reminiscent of a time when, you suspect, true craftsmanship was valued a little more highly than it is today. The good news is that in the right hands and right places, it is a highly efficient tool - certainly a match for any other rod, but that much more fun to fish with. And that is really important. Fun is what fishing should be. I don't say this out loud, for fear of incurring another of Nick's *looks*. I know he doesn't approve of my choice of tackle. I know he thinks I'm handicapping myself. I *am* beginning to feel my age…!

Nick explains that this is a complex river to fish, and it needs to be approached with both commitment and flexibility. Hence the need for a longer 'technical' rod.

Oh dear, and I thought I was just going *fishing*!

I try to concentrate on his words of wisdom, but my focus is wavering. That view across the river valley really *is* spectacular; the sounds of the river, insects and birds makes my heart sing. Confirmation, if any were needed, as to why I am a fisherman.

Nick offers to lend me one of his rods but I decline – graciously, I hope - and say that if I struggle then I will take him up on his kind offer. I suspect that his definition of the word 'struggle' probably involves more fish in the net than mine does. I pull on my boots and start to fasten my knee pads. *"Where are your chest waders?"* Nick asks, a touch of hysteria creeping into his voice…

"I thought I would just start off with the boots and knee pads," I tell him. "I often find that by keeping low and moving slow I can pick off the odd fish close into the bank".

"That's fine, but you will catch a *lot* more by deep wading. There are loads of fish in this river to be caught, but you'll never reach them with that set-up. Give me a shout when you're ready and I'll help you set up properly."

As I watch Nick head down to the river, I suspect he's given up on me. I feel a slight sense of relief. It doesn't seem so long ago that my own approach to fishing wasn't that different to Nick's. Like most of us, when I first started fishing all I wanted to do was catch a fish - any fish, regardless of size. Later, once I had fished for a while, I wanted to catch lots of fish, and then, later still, the *biggest* fish. Now, the advancing years have brought me to a level of contentment that allows me to take a more relaxed approach to various of aspects of my life, not just my fishing. What is important to me now is *how* I catch my fish – matters of numbers and size have become less important as the years have gone by. What really matters is my *approach* to fishing and, although it may appear rather quaint to some, the methods and tackle I use are integral to my enjoyment - even if it is at the expense of the fish in the net.

Once Nick is gone, I wander down to the river and look for a good place to start – preferably a spot with a rising fish or two and plenty of bank-side cover. But nothing is showing. For a while I just sit in the long grass and wait…

There! I see nothing, but I'm sure I heard a fish rise. I sit quietly; relaxed yet alert, trying to tune in to all my senses to locate the fish. Minutes pass and all remains quiet. The fish hasn't revealed itself. I feel myself beginning to drift into a dreamlike state; the day has warmed up, the clouds are low and the wind has dropped. All the elements seem to be conspiring to send me to sleep; I'm not used to these early starts.

Suddenly, there it is again! I instantly see the slowly dispersing rings of the rise. Quickly but carefully, I raise myself up on my knees, unhook the Daddy Long Legs from the keeper ring and make the short cast of about fifteen feet to where I estimate the fish to be positioned. The fly is taken in a violent rise the moment it hits the surface of the water. I play the fish carefully, staying on my knees and trying to keep myself below the horizon so as not to alarm the trout any more than necessary. It's a beautiful brown trout; not my biggest from a river, but still a very good fish. I quickly unhook it in the net and watch it swim off with a violent flick of its tail, spraying me in a welcome shower of cool river water. I lie back contentedly in the long grass, cocooned by the foliage and the heavy press of the atmosphere. I quickly drift off into a deep, welcome sleep…

"Steve!"

Nick's voice fragments my dreams and instantly I'm awake. "How have you done? Pretty well I imagine if you've got time for a snooze!" I fudge my answer and say I'm happy with my results.

"I've had eleven including a couple of Grayling, but it hasn't been easy. They've all been lying quite deep - most took a peeping caddis".

"What's been your most successful fly?" Nick asks. Truthfully, I disclose it's been the 'daddy'. My answer makes Nick suspicious. "I can't say that I've seen much surface activity" he retorts with a questioning look. I mumble something about targeting opportunistic feeders and, changing the subject, propose that we have a bite to eat.

After lunch, Nick suggests that we try a change of tactics. He'll lend me his rod and guide me for the rest of the day. He tells me I need to put a few more fish in the net. It's clear this is an offer I can't refuse and so, after struggling into my chest waders, I follow Nick upstream to commence my tuition in the dark art of 'Euro Nymphing'. Nick proves to be an excellent coach and soon I'm wading deep and hooking fish that I didn't even know were there! We catch lots and I finish the day admitting having hooked and landed as many fish as I have ever caught in an afternoons' fishing.

On the drive home I try to explain to Nick (without sounding ungrateful) that while I'd had a great time, the one fish I'd caught in the morning gave me more satisfaction than the many fish I caught later in the day. As I said, it's *how* I catch my fish that matters to me, more and more so as the years pass. I thank Nick for taking me to such a good place and for opening my eyes to new methods and techniques newly added to my fly-fishing repertoire and try to reassure him that I've had a really good day. I refrain from explaining how I worry about the damage being done to the riverbed by the increasing numbers of deep-wading anglers anxious to 'bag up' and improve on their personal bests in number and size. I know I'm in danger of sounding 'holier-than-thou', and recognise the fact that if I were thirty years younger I, too, would be fishing the same methods as Nick and his friends. But I believe it's a good thing for many parts of the river to be inaccessible to me with my more traditional approach. The fish, like us, need safe places - sanctuary, if you will. They must also have their "good places", places we cannot disturb them. Always remember, the trout that is out of reach today may by tomorrow have moved into a position where it *can* be caught. It is this uncertainty and anticipation that keeps me fishing and coming back for more - and I love it!

So, if one day you find me dozing in the long grass by the river, with my cane rod at my side and no chest waders in sight (just boots and knee pads!), leave me be and know that I am in a "good place" of my own…

PS. You may be interested to know that a couple of weeks later I did treat myself to a more *'technical'* rod; ten foot, not eleven and Boron rather than Carbon... Oh, and a new reel to go with it! Well, you never know, do you? All I need now is a good place to try it out. Perhaps I'll give Nick a call...

PPS. Last night, I had a dream... my old cane rods had me surrounded and each, in turn, beat and poked at me, taunting me with regard to the fact that my seduction and betrayal was complete and then, along with several large trout, pursued me, chasing me from the river and chanting in unison; *'there's no fool like an old fool...'*

The new rod remains in its tube in the corner - unused.

75

Just Add Water

(Recipe for a perfect day)

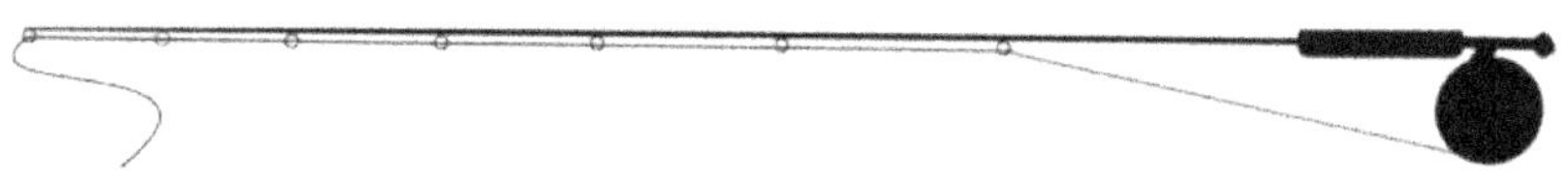

Blend the aroma of Wild Garlic, gently crushed under
random foot, with a hint of freshly mown hay.
Mix with Dog Rose, Wild Orchid or Purple Loosestrife,
In quantities to please the eye.
Dust with dance of Iron Blue Dun or Yellow May,
Accompanied by a soft cadence of birdsong.
Season to taste.
(Ideally late spring - but at a pinch, early autumn)
Slowly warm for several hours under an English sun
(If available)
Fanning occasionally with a gentle, cooling breeze.
Add water.
(Preferably sparkling and chilled)
Finally,
(After allowing to soak until it rises)
Take one Trout, fat as butter
Its golden flanks peppered with scarlet moles.
Drain, before re-soaking.
Serve at least once a week.

<u>WARNING</u>: *if you are lucky, this recipe may repeat on you!*

Snake In the Grass

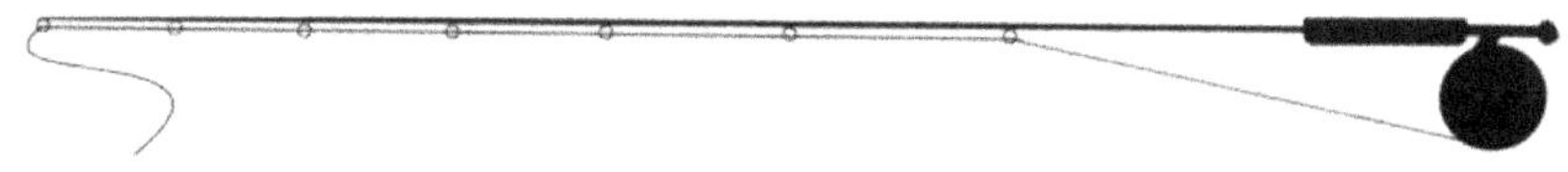

They say it's one of the few creatures that, when threatened, rolls over and plays dead.

The trouble is, I don't think this particular one felt threatened. They also say that before it *does* roll over, it may puff up its body and emit a foul-smelling liquid all over its aggressor.

This information, had I known it at the time, would have proved useful.

As it was, up until this moment, my knowledge and experience of snakes was sketchy at best. Being British, I hadn't really felt it necessary to acquaint myself with the personal habits of a reptile usually associated with jungles, deserts and swamps. The last place I expected to meet one was in the benign English chalk-stream in which I now stood…

The day had started off well enough. We had arrived at the Kennet - near Hungerford - with the intention of catching a few of the big, wild browns which inhabit the narrow carriers of the main river. On my way to the carrier, just above the weir in the main river, I was distracted by the swirl of what looked like a good fish. The Kennet at this point is particularly wide, and the fish was beyond the limits of my casting ability. Since I was wearing thigh waders, I cautiously waded out towards the centre of the river until the water's surface was within a whisker of my wader tops. I stood motionless; waiting for the fish to rise again, and eventually it did. With a heavily greased Spider pattern, the fish took my first cast. As soon as I struck, I realised it wasn't actually a trout at all, but a superb chub of around 4lb. I brought it to hand and released it.

Just as I was about to wade back to the bank, a movement in the water caught my eye. My first thought was that it must have been a rodent of some kind. To my horror, I realised the creature was a snake! Not *just* a snake, however, but a snake of about five feet in length; swimming directly at me! My blood ran cold, and I quickly calculated that the snake's course, if maintained, would lead directly to my wader tops! I was convinced they would look like the entrance to a nice dark hole – just perfect for an evil, slippery serpent to make its own!

With my body frozen by the horror of my situation, my brain worked overtime on how to escape. Do I remain motionless and hope the snake will change course? Do I make a run for the bank? At best, my waders would fill with water. At worst, I may stumble - giving the snake the chance to do goodness knows what! Suddenly and instinctively, I slapped the surface of the water with my trusty old Sharpes Fario. The snake stopped. Again, I brought my rod down hard on the surface and let out a yell in the best Tarzan tradition! The snake turned and dived! In a blind panic, I stumbled towards the bank - waders now full of water - before struggling to lift myself out of the river to catch my breath and regain my composure.

I did fish on for a few hours but couldn't shake the uneasy feeling that something… somewhere… was watching me. The hunter had become the hunted…

Since this harrowing experience, I have only ever encountered the same type of grass snake on one other occasion. This time, however, I calmly watched it swim across Kennick Reservoir before it disappeared into the long grass. Again, this specimen was about five feet in length - although they *can* grow longer. If you should ever come across one, it is useful to know that they are generally a grey-green shade, with black spots and a yellowish creamy-orange collar. Bearing in mind their predilection for damp habitats (especially riverbanks, ponds and ditches), I'm surprised fishermen don't encounter them more frequently, considering they are active during the day and like to bask in the sun.

You will be relieved to learn, however, that anglers do not form a major part of their diet. They prefer tadpoles, frogs, newts, mice, fish and even small birds; although most of their hunting is done underwater, and their prey swallowed alive. If you do happen to encounter one, don't assume just because it dives when disturbed that it has gone. Grass snakes can stay submerged for up to an hour - so that feeling of not being alone may have been more than just a feeling. But in the improbable event that one *does* find its way into your waders, you'll be glad to hear that its venom is not harmful to humans. Though I suspect the atmosphere inside the average fisherman's waders may well be hazardous to snakes...!

Future-Proof

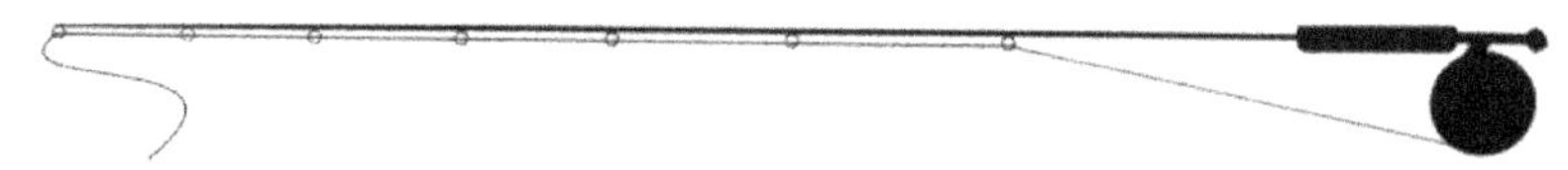

Some people say I've given up and given in. That I'm no longer on the ball. I like to think I've matured. I admit that there was once a time when I eagerly awaited the arrival of the latest tackle catalogues. I admit I spent a small fortune on all the latest gadgets. High modulus rods, reels with braking systems which wouldn't be out of place on a Porsche - all of these things and more, were mine. I also admit that I lost sight of what first attracted me to fishing; simply connecting with a wild creature in wild surroundings. Guilty as charged.

As the years progressed, the insidious soft-focus hype of the marketing men obscured the truth and I came to believe that in order to be successful and really enjoy my fishing, I must have the latest equipment. I was so blinded, I couldn't see that in most cases the latest wonder-product didn't perform any differently from the tackle I already possessed! My corruption was total and expensive, in that as sure as night follows day, new rod followed new rod, new reel followed new reel and new line followed new line. What I *couldn't* see was that my focus had shifted away from the fishing itself, to the high gloss of the tackle. I believed that unless I had the latest 'premium' gear, then my 'experience' would be somehow incomplete. The tackle industry had caught me, "hook, line and sinker!"

Perhaps it was the fact it was taking me longer and longer to get ready to fish that I eventually started to think. Every trip, I would struggle into my lightweight breathable chest waders, fiddle interminably with braces, belts, buckles, gravel guards and laces before donning a waistcoat so laden with tackle, my shoulders ached before I even got down to the river! I would then ponder on which line to use - double taper or weight forward? Floater or sink tip? Maybe an intermediate, or even a fast sinker…

Perhaps it was because, despite having all this latest technology at my fingertips, I was actually enjoying my fishing less and less, beginning to daydream of the simpler fishing I loved so much as a boy; the fishing that had seduced me and given me so many enchanting childhood experiences and memories. Perhaps I was becoming a victim of nostalgia, but I was convinced that my happiest recollections stemmed from those simpler times, even though the fish were fewer and smaller.

Then, I saw the light! Despite possessing all the tackle and technology I could ever want, I had lost my way. The romance of fly fishing had been lost to me, and we all know what happens once the romance has disappeared from a relationship! This simple realisation was my epiphany…

On the small-to-medium-sized rivers that I normally fished, I had found that by wearing chest waders and using the latest technical rods, reels and lines - even for an angler of my limited casting skills - there were few, if any, parts of the river that could not be fished. If a trout was rising, one way or another, I could put a fly over it. There was no hiding place for the fish, or for me if I failed to catch. It could only be down to my lack of skill. The prospect of a blank day was unthinkable.

From this point on, my 'road to Damascus' was easily travelled.

The first thing I did, despite what my wife may think, was to rationalise my collection of tackle. I now mainly fish with a light cane rod and a simple reel loaded with a floating line - what some might call "classic" tackle. (Mrs. Murgatroyd, having just read the above and relishing both the irony of the situation and my ability to convince myself of anything if it suits my agenda, insists that I point out the cost of this 'simple' outfit is roughly *three times* that of a quality carbon rod!).

Wherever possible, I now tend to fish predominately with dry flies. I usually wear wellingtons or thigh waders in place of the 'chesties,' and carry my small box of flies, floatant and knife either in my pockets or in a small fishing bag.

Now of course, there are many parts of the river I cannot cover, and lots of rising fish tantalisingly out of reach, but I don't care! I now once again love my fishing as much as I used to! I leave the river hoping that the big fish that was out of my reach today, may tomorrow have moved within range.

I find that I now often just laze by the river after catching a fish and enjoy the sights and sounds, while I wait for the Kelly Kettle to boil; just being at 'one' with nature. I no longer fish frantically from dawn to dusk, as I so often did, usually leaving with a headache. No. I sit and watch the world go by. Now just one wild fish is enough to satisfy me, and that sense of wonder has made a welcome return to my fishing, along with the anticipation of the next trip and the next fish...

Many may think that by taking this route I am limiting my fishing - - but I believe that, through this *simpler* approach, I have rediscovered the magic and romance that for a while seemed to elude me.

Some people still tell me I've given up and given in - that I'm living in the past. I just tell them I'm future-proof!

The Stalker

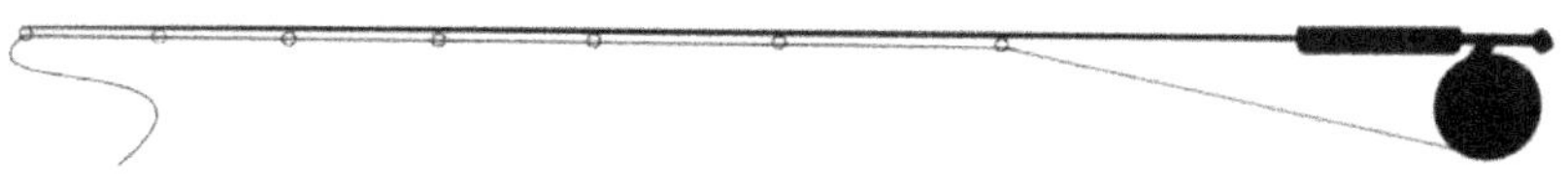

I watched you from the bank
You didn't know I was there
I saw your slender body; graceful, unaware.
I watched you move
I watched you browse
I watched you take your time
I watched you 'till I knew that one day you'd be mine.

Every day I think of you
Your brown skin and dark eyes
Imagine how you'll feel to me, vibrant and alive.
I watched you rest
I watched you eat
I watched you fill your days
I watched you and I waited, studying your ways.

Although you've never seen me
One day I know you will
Now I've got your number, your routine and your drill.
I'll see you come; I'll see you go; I'll see you won't forget;
I'll see you one day soon, in the bottom of my net.

A Rod of Distinction

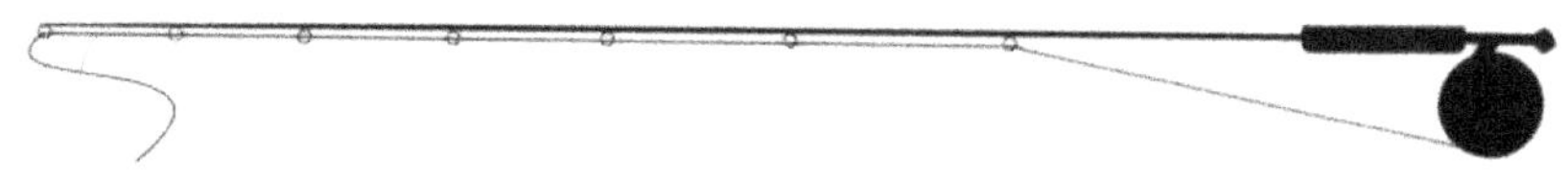

Ari 't Hart has cost me a lot of money over the years...
I don't remember when I first became aware of his reels. Like many things, it was probably a gradual, growing awareness there was something special out there. Something to aspire to. Something to be coveted. As always, *money* was the problem! As the years passed, however, finances gradually improved. Suddenly, there is the realisation you're spending an unhealthy amount of time searching the internet for yet *another* reel to add to your already ample collection...!

It was during one of these routine online searches that a certain rod appeared. The listing referred to it as an *'Ari 't Hart' Rod*. One of only four or five ever made! It was 8' in length, and rated 4/5. The finish was a stunning translucent grey with a distinctive Hart reel seat. The maker was Marcus Warwick.

Of course, I *had* to have it - - and thus began my love affair with his *"Rods of Distinction"*.

I had always been aware of Marcus as a maker of fly-rods; indeed, I remember reading glowing reviews, and seeing his adverts in Brian Harris' 'International Flyfisher' magazine amongst others. But again, being a student at the time, the thought of actually owning one was out of the question. The rod duly arrived, and it was beautifully finished. I was intrigued by the claim it was only one of a handful ever built, so I decided to write to Marcus for more information. Sadly, I was just too late; Marcus had recently passed away (September, 2012). His widow, Jocelyn, gave my letter to Richard Holman, a close friend and 'protege' (and now an established maker in his own right). Richard kindly replied, supplying me with a huge amount of information regarding not only the rod in question, but also many other Warwick rods. It is to my great regret that I was never able to meet the man himself, but Richard paints a great picture of him:

For ten years or more during the nineteen-eighties and nineties, I saw a lot of Marcus Warwick - who many people will remember as a huge character, and a fine fisherman and rod-maker who enjoyed an international reputation. We lived in the same town (Uppingham in Rutland), and he agreed to mentor me while I learned how to make split bamboo fly rods. As I was considerably younger than Marcus, it was inevitable that our relationship became that of pupil and teacher and, being a little over-eager, I would constantly badger him with questions! At the time, I had no idea of the complexity of the questions for which I would expect an obvious and straightforward answer. On one such occasion, I innocently asked: 'How can you tell which bamboo culm will make a good rod?'

It is a measure of the man that he never turned me away. Instead, he invited me to his workshop to receive some sage advice. He lived not much more than a few hundred yards from my house, but a visit to Marcus' somehow seemed like taking a longer journey - a journey into the world of a man who never lost his pre-war Hungarian roots - a world of Slavic enthusiasms, zest for life and old-world European charm. Anyone who has met Marcus would know exactly what I mean!

On this evening, I found myself entering the gates of Marcus' house and waving across the courtyard at the kindly face with flowing hair which was illuminated by the light of the window of his workshop. "Hello Richard," the robust, Hungarian voice sounded out, "Come in and we'll talk."

Marcus' workshop was the stuff of dreams. Stone built, with an area for ageing and drying bamboo on the first floor and the main working area below. It was full of fantastic machinery which offered his customers tantalising glimpses of objects of desire and the arcane processes of the craftsman.

His workshop was the physical manifestation of the man himself - sophistication rubbing shoulders with the homespun. A milling machine, tuned to cut strips of cane to tolerances of thousandths of an inch, traversed one end of the room, whilst in a corner a stained pine wardrobe, of the sort described as "utility" just after the War, served as his varnish drying cabinet.

The evening started with a whiskey. Then his lesson began. It surprised me that he talked about everything but rod making: import duties; currency conversion; VAT; politics; horse racing; the price of fish (yes, literally the price of fish); shooting; recipes; literature; wildlife; travel; more recipes - Marcus was a man of infinite and eclectic interests and, like many autodidacts, his knowledge randomly followed his passions. Every few minutes he poured another dram.

Marcus sat at his bench which ran alongside a south facing window which gave him a view of his walled garden, the kitchen of his house and any signals that might be communicated from there by his wife Jocelyn. Like all the best workbenches it had a place for everything but nothing was in its place. Its surface was covered in containers of various kinds, each with a handwritten note sitting on top. (Marcus had an enviably beautiful script which adorned each of his handcrafted rods.)

In numerous Romeo y Julieta cigar humidifiers he kept his rare silks: Belding and Cortecelli 00 in all the classic American rod maker colours, particularly Payne Brown as he considered Jim Payne to be the greatest of them all. Then boxes from Watsons of Leek containing silk from Perivale, Pearsalls and Elephant Brand in clarets, greens and golds. In wine boxes were his first selection of Portuguese flor grade cork shives imported from Señor Joao Jose Figueiras dos Santos.

Eventually, he came around to fishing and rod making: "Ari's reels are still years ahead in design…"; "I met Hoagy at Chatsworth that year…"; Jim Hardy sent me that taper, it's the genuine Marvel …" Marcus made a huge number of fine rods during his career but I think that his true joy came from the people he met through his rod making. He spent hours typing out long communications to send to customers and contacts all around the world.

When we'd drunk several more whiskies and he considered that we had journeyed enough around the world of rod making, the culm of Tonkin cane, heavy and golden, appeared. He'd not forgotten my question after all. He weighed it in his hands and looked at it like a

Over the intervening years, Richard and I have continued our friendship and, with his guidance and advice, he has assisted me in building up a treasured collection of some of Marcus' more distinctive rods. His bamboo rods are sublime, and are available on the second-hand market at surprisingly affordable prices.

As a bespoke maker, Marcus very often made "one-off" rods to match the requirements of individual customers. He also had a few favourite tapers of his own, made as his standards, often calling these his *"Sniper"* rods. His personal preference was for a tip-inclined dry fly action. Two of the best tapers were his seven-foot rod for a 4-weight line, and a three-piece eight-foot-five weight rod - one of which he made for his friend, Hoagy Carmichael. Marcus described his approach to rod design as being "practical and empirical," rather than theoretical... Often, his rods were based on his own versions of classic rods he'd measured when they came into his workshop for repair - or were adaptations of published tapers. He was quite able to improve on the fishability of these designs based on his own experience.

One of these was a seven-footer derived from a rod called the *"Sylph"*, designed by Wes Jordon (who became a rod designer for Orvis) and produced by the American firm of Cross. It was marketed "the sportiest rod ever built." It was very lightweight in its construction, and deceptively powerful. The taper for the rod was published in *"Herter's Professional Secrets of Fishing Rods and How Fishing Rods are Made",* and a very similar taper made its way across the pond to Richard Walker's *"Rod Building for Amateurs"*. Which book was the source for Marcus is not sure, but he was able to develop and produce a rod that became a firm favourite among his customers.

Interestingly - and somewhat surprisingly – is that while his bamboo rods compare with the best, it is in some of his carbon rods that his inventiveness and originality shines through.

At a time when the tackle trade was dominated by the big manufacturers, Marcus carved a very successful niche for himself. In addition to his bespoke work, he also marketed a range of truly unique rods - filling a gap in the market.

Charles McLaren (famed Sea Trout angler and author) commissioned Marcus to produce a 12-foot 6-weight rod with a 6" extension handle. The rod proved such a success that Marcus added it to his range. I own an example, and it fishes beautifully. In addition to the standard handle, it has a double-handed butt - - making it possibly the first-ever Switch rod!

My most treasured (and probably most used) of his rods is the *'Globetrotter'* -- a travel rod with a difference. This is Marcus' own description: *"...it is uniquely two rods in one. Having two butt sections among its seven pieces, the owner can assemble either an 8' 6" Isabella or a 7' Maria fly rod in high modulus chestnut-coloured carbon..."*

The rod was also available in a mahogany presentation box, part of a production run of only seventy. In addition to the rod, the set included a wooden fly box stocked with a large selection of American and European dry flies, along with an Ari 't Hart 'Columbus' fly reel - a reel most collectors are likely unaware of...

Marcus exemplified everything an independent craftsman should be. Each rod was individually made for a particular customer, conversations and correspondence prefacing their manufacture. Anyone who found their way to his home and workshop to discuss their requirements would be warmly welcomed and entertained. Marcus' knowledge and experience would help steer his clients towards which rods and tackle would be best-suited individually to them, and the kind of fishing they intended it for. He was very keen that customers would leave him with a balanced and appropriate outfit.

The life of an independent rod-maker is not an easy one. Uncertain and unpredictable, quality *still* shines through; clients often becoming loyal friends to Marcus, going back time and again for more rods… or simply to listen to him talk.

A man of distinction.

marcuswarwick.co.uk

Steven Murgatroyd & Richard Holman

Chasing the Dragon

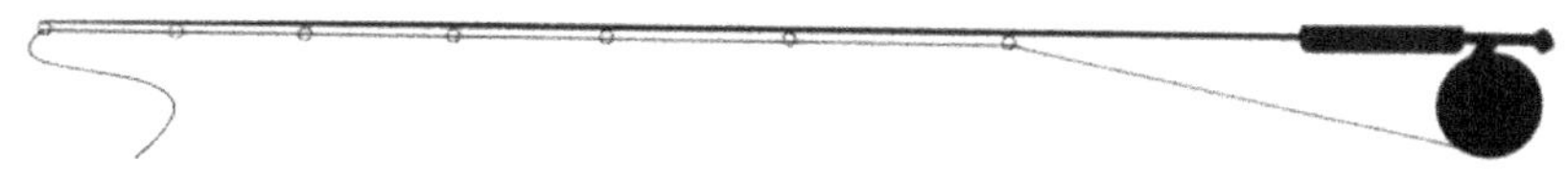

Just one more "last cast"… This one really *will* be the last. I wait and watch… there - a rise! I freeze, willing the fish to again betray its presence. I realise I'm holding my breath in an attempt to conceal myself. But just as living its life inevitably reveals the whereabouts of the fish, I cannot deny the adrenalin now coursing through my body; from my heart to my fingertips - the rhythmic pulsing of the rod tip telegraphing *my* position to the surrounding world.

I stare into the glare of the water's surface, searching for a sign. Just one more cast… I should have been back over an hour ago… but here's a chance to save the day… a chance to score…

The world closes in on me. Nothing exists outside the egocentric bubble I have created. It's just me… and the trout… All of my senses are tuned in to pinpointing the lie of the fish. I know I'll have only one shot at this. Slowly, I remove the fly from the keeper ring and blow on it. There! The fish rises again… and again! Working carefully, I draw line from the reel; aerialise what I judge to be just enough, and let the cast go. Time stands still. Just let me hook this one fish, *please*; then I'll go… *just one fish…*that's all I want, that's all I need …*please!*

The need – no - the *craving* to feed this addiction began when I was at school. The river Clwyd was a short bike ride (or a long walk!) away from home and, for a few years, I would fish two or three days a week there after school. If a week went by without catching a trout then I believed I was losing my touch, that I could not rightly call myself a fisherman. An obsession, everybody assumed, that I would *surely* grow out of; no one suspecting for one moment that this was an obsession that would grow insidiously into addiction.

The fly gently alights on the water's surface about twelve inches upstream of the trout's last rise. My world has slowed to a series of silent, stuttering freeze-frames as the fly inches its way ever-closer towards the trout. Breathing is, again, involuntarily suspended as an uncontrollable trembling telegraphs my anxiety down the line and into the river. *Please, please* take, I promise I will let you go and then pack up – I *promise!*

In my heart of hearts, I know the outcome is academic. Like all addicts, I will return again and again - making the same promises, saying the same selfish prayers… and never really wanting to be free of my obsession.

Borrowed Time

A Cautionary Tale

"When I was a boy, fly fishing was magical and my rod was a wand that cast flies over the river and spells over me". Wilbury flashed a contemptuous glance in my direction, his bright blue eyes steely in their expression before rolling towards the heavens from under his bramble-like brows. He shuffled his tired boots and let out a world-weary sigh.

"Your trouble is that you live in the past. You were naïve as a kid and you and your lot are naïve now. You're all on borrowed time!" And with that, Wilbury slumped down into the old leather armchair in the corner of the hut, closed his eyes and ignored me. I sat at the fly-tying bench, pondering his words, trying to tease out the thread of truth that ran through them and tie it into the consciousness of my own experience.

Foot and mouth frustration had finally forced me back to the still waters; the river benefiting from the 'windfall' break. The closed season had now encompassed virtually all four seasons, giving the riverside footpaths (formally rough scars of earth) time to heal as Mother Nature systematically eradicated any sign of man. Wilbury suddenly snorted in his sleep — the same snort that he'd thrown at me when I had told him I was going to visit the local 'put-and-take' fishery. He had warned me I was making a mistake. He had warned me I was betraying the trout I claimed to hold so dear. He had warned me that my fellow fishermen and I would pay a high price if we did not change our ways…

On my arrival at the fishery, I parked my car next to the stews; the water's surface boiling in response to the agitation of the anxious trout. I queued to buy my ticket before setting off to secure the best fishing platform — trying to hide my haste from my fellow consumers. I spent most of the day sitting, watching and waiting. All around me rooted automatons cast and retrieved with a monotony reminiscent of a production line. They had all paid their money. They had all caught fish.

The favourite and most killing technique used was akin to teasing a cat with a scrap of wool. The philosophy appearing to be: "Pull it past its nose often enough, and eventually it'll pounce!" With a growing sense of unease, I made my escape. On my way home I decided to make a detour via the only stretch of river that remained accessible. Not to fish. Just to wish...

The track down to the river is steep. The car rocks violently as you slowly negotiate the ruts and potholes. The suburban tyres slide as they struggle to get a grip on the unfamiliar earth. As you cross a small ancient bridge the tunnel of lush foliage through which you have been travelling suddenly opens up revealing the bright sky. The sudden increase in light lifts your spirits and fills you with hope and anticipation. If you do decide to fish you may catch perhaps just one wild fish. Later you might lay for a while under a tree — cocooned in the long grass — no longer an intruder on the scene — but now part of it. With luck you will encounter no other human beings.

Wilbury awoke with a start, launching into a severe coughing fit, spraying spittle in all directions! He grabbed my hip flask and allowed most of its contents to calm his cough.

"You're right," I said. "As long as we treat fish as a disposable commodity, we're leaving ourselves wide open to criticism from groups and organisations who would like to see fishing banned."

"Hallelujah, I'll drink to that!" coughed Wilbury.

"But I think *you're* the one being naïve now!" I said. "You're suggesting there are enough wild places and wild fish to satisfy the vast number of fishermen around today!" Wilbury fixed me with one of his looks, lifted himself out of the chair and breathed a mist of whisky fumes in my direction.

"Not!" he barked. "If you change your values, broaden your horizons and get real."

"Real?" I looked at him, puzzled.

"Real" he repeated, rolling the 'R' around his mouth before firing the word at me.

Finally, I recognised the truth in his words. I had already realised that for my fishing to mean anything more to me, my quarry must be wild — caught in wild places. *That* is where the satisfaction lies, not in the size of a fish or the numbers caught. And there are lots of opportunities for the fly fisherman. There are Bass, Pollack and Mackerel to be caught from the shore; Pike and Perch in the lakes; and Grayling, Chub and Dace in many of our rivers. All you need is imagination. I turned to look again at Wilbury, but he had gone. I stepped through the doorway and out into the twilight. I looked towards the woods, and for a moment I imagined that I saw him. He paused, looked back at me and smiled, before raising my hip flask to his lips and merging magically into the shadows.

The Non-Smoker's Guide to Catching More Trout

It was a small Welsh market town that had probably seen better days. It was set amongst glorious rolling open pastureland, cradled on all sides by a range of impressive geographic features that you would find difficult to describe as mountains without giving the impression that you didn't get out much, but still too grand to be dismissed as 'just hills'. The town wasn't as poor as some in the Principality by any stretch of the imagination; cushioned as it was by the annual influx of tourists, attracted by its sandstone castle and elevated market square – itself flanked on all sides by quaint Tudor buildings. In the late '60s, however, its range of shops was limited, by and large, to the essential - many shops combining two or more businesses under one roof, in order to make ends meet.

One such shop was the local newsagents. Set just off the squarc, it sold everything you might expect a newsagent and tobacconist to sell in those simpler days, along with a number of other goods that, presumably, demand dictated. Kettles, light bulbs, penknives and hairbrushes are some of the items I recall. The shop boasted two large picture windows, which displayed various dusty, sun-bleached goods. There was also a third, smaller window which demanded my attention every time I passed by…

A few hundred yards down the hill from the shop, just beyond the cafe, the car park and the public toilets, lay the river. A trout river. When we first moved to the town, I don't think I had ever seen a trout that wasn't just a picture in a book.

Come to think of it, I don't think I had even seen one on a dinner plate. I did, however, consider myself a fisherman - not that I had caught very much at that stage in my life (some may say, with an element of truth, that little has changed). My only tackle was a bright green seven-foot Milbro; a solid glass spinning rod acquired with numerous books of Green Shield stamps. But that didn't matter. It was a start, and I was determined to become a trout fisherman. And I was going to catch them the *proper* way - with a fly.

The problem was, I didn't know anyone who fished - never mind fly-fished! I wasn't a member of the club and didn't know how to join. In addition, I didn't have the right tackle. But I had *seen* the right tackle. It was in that third window of Mr. Roberts' newsagent shop. And what's more, it was Hardy tackle; the tackle of choice, the tackle of Royalty, the tackle of experts and - somewhat depressingly - the tackle of the wealthy. Still, where there's a will...

Fortuitously, my mother had recently opened a dress shop in the town, and my father had joined the local 'Round Table.' As a result, they made the acquaintance of 'Roberts the News,' and just happened to mention to him their son's desperation to learn how to catch a trout on a fly. With an eye to a sale - but also, I like to think, because he loved his fishing and recognised within my enthusiasm a fledgeling kindred spirit – Mr. Roberts agreed that once an outfit had been purchased, he would enrol me in the club and take me to the river to show me the ropes.

My parents weren't wealthy and knew nothing of fishing. However, whether by luck, judgement, or skilful salesmanship on the part of 'Roberts the News' (probably a touch of each), my first fly rod was duly purchased. A Hardy Jet; seven-and-a-half feet of rich, dark brown glass, built to take a five-weight line. It was, at the time, the most beautiful and exciting thing I had ever seen, and is still - to this day - one of my most prized possessions. Obviously, the budget didn't run to a Hardy reel to match. The little Intrepid reel, however, was more than adequate. Some fifty years later, it's proudly displayed up on the shelf above me as I write. It has lost some of its paint and also sports a few scratches - all testament to the long and bumpy road to achieving fly fishing mediocrity. The path I was about to embark upon when I first removed the reel from its box and tentatively attached it to my new rod.

The appointed day duly arrived, and I was collected by Mr. Roberts and driven down to the river. I was shown how to set up my tackle. A level leader was attached to the end of the floating fly line by way of a rudimentary knot and loop arrangement, and some kind of wet fly was attached to the other end. Mr. Roberts told me that he stocked a couple of publications by Hardy in his shop that would teach me the basics if I studied them. Of course, I bought them, and they each became my bibles over the next couple of years. I was briefly shown the rudiments of a basic overhead cast, and then we picked up our bags and headed towards the river.

At last, I was a *proper angler* - a *fly fisherman*. The fact that I hadn't actually caught a trout never crossed my mind. I had achieved what I had been dreaming of for what seemed like years and, with the naivety of youth, I assumed that catching a trout would simply be a natural progression. Little did I realise that frustrations and disappointments lay ahead. I think we anglers are generally optimists at heart. It is that quest for the elusive that drives us on and keeps us returning time and time again, certain that we are about to achieve success. It is only with the passing years that our definition of success is refined and honed, as we realise that true success is not measured in the numbers or size of fish that we catch. It is measured in the way we conduct ourselves; in our respect for our quarry and surroundings and also in the pure joy, contentment with (and appreciation of) the places that a fly rod can take you. Of course, I would be the last to deny that a few fish along the way helps with all of this - and the truth is that, without the fish, we might all be doing something more socially acceptable with our days. Playing golf, perhaps...
Thank God for the trout.

As we approached the river, Mr. Roberts motioned me to slow down, crouch down and calm down. He led me towards a fallen tree trunk some twenty feet or so from the riverbank and quietly suggested that I sit with him while he smoked a cigarette. Our position afforded a good view of a nice pool just below a small natural weir. I sat with a growing sense of frustration as a battered and scratched tobacco tin was produced from the pocket of an old tweed jacket before Mr. Roberts - with discoloured, yellowed fingertips - proceeded to slowly and deliberately roll himself a cigarette. For what seemed like an age, we both sat in a haze of pungent smoke; Mr. Roberts studying the pool, me becoming more and more restless. At one point, I suggested that I was going down to the river to start fishing, but my mentor silently raised his arm to signal that I was to stay where I was. Eventually and mercifully, the cigarette was gone. Mr. Roberts slowly rose to his feet. In my excitement, I started to follow him, only to be told to stay where I was. Keeping low, he approached the bank. When he was still a good six feet from the water's edge, he knelt and peeled a few yards of line from his reel before casting his fly towards the river - no false casting, as little movement as possible; the whole procedure was executed with an air of serenity. It was an almost dreamlike sequence of events that followed: The fly was on the water for no more than a few seconds before I saw the rod tip raised, the water exploding as an unsuspecting trout realised it was hooked. Unable to contain my excitement, I ran to the water's edge and watched in awe as the fish was netted. It was the first live trout that I had ever seen, and I had seen it caught on a fly. To my innocent young eyes, it all looked so easy.

I never accompanied Mr. Roberts to the river again. He said that he had shown me all I needed to know in order to get started. In retrospect, I now appreciate that he *had*; even though I failed to recognise this at the time. I subsequently made numerous trips to the river and had many blanks before finally catching my first fish, and many more blanks to come before catching my second. I just hadn't taken in what Mr.

Roberts had demonstrated to me. On my solo outings, I would be full of excitement and enthusiasm. I didn't want to waste a moment of my precious fishing time. Of course, I would go straight to the water's edge on my arrival and attempt - by way of numerous false casts and wading where possible - to get my fly as close to the far bank as possible. I now realise that any fish that may have been in the vicinity when I arrived at the river were long gone before I even got my fly on the water.

The problem is my being a non-smoker. I thought Mr. Roberts just wanted a smoke before he started fishing. He did, of course, but he also used his time by the riverside to *study* the water; something I now know will pay dividends in the form of a much higher catch rate. Now, I'm not suggesting that smoking is good for you - or your fishing - but sitting discreetly by the waterside when you arrive at a new pool or run definitely is! It is also good for your soul and your disposition; not only will you feel calmer and more at one with your surroundings, you will also start to see things that previously you would have missed, including fish. None of us, I am sure, spend enough time just *watching* and *waiting* by the riverside. In fact, I would go so far as to say that it's *impossible* to spend too much time on this! Keep movement to a minimum, try not to wade - at least until you have explored the margins - wear drab clothing, avoid shiny tackle that can, on a bright day, semaphore your presence from a long way off. Act like the predator you are and, where possible, conceal your presence. Keep below the horizon. If you are a smoker you will, no doubt, find the watching and waiting easier... If not, heed Walton's advice – 'study to be quiet.' Chewing gum might help - maybe even a cup of coffee, but perhaps not baccy...!

Instant Karma

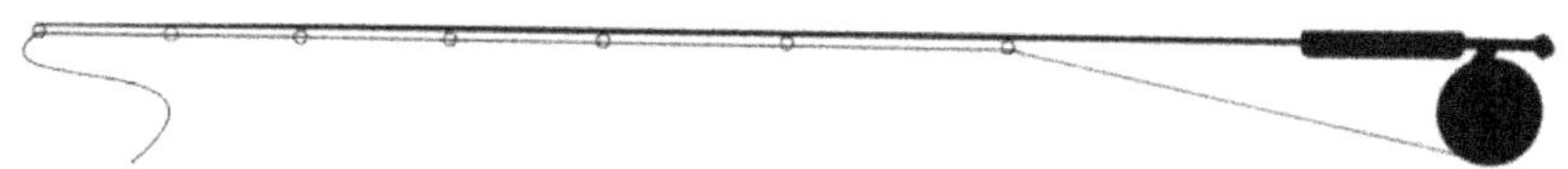

In an old ex-GPO Morris Minor van (still painted pillar-box red), "Mike the Milk" and I, under cover of darkness, followed a tight and twisting track deep into the Welsh hills. With unfamiliar tackle – no rod; just waders, a landing net and a torch – the destination remained unknown, to me at least.

For the last quarter of a mile, despite being blind in one eye, Mike dimmed the headlights. For what seemed like an age, he cautiously edged his way down an old farm track before finally killing the engine. The new silence revealed the sound of a nearby stream. Few words were spoken. Mike led; I followed. We made our way through the damp grass, down the bank and then into the stream. The icy water gripped my legs, and the darkness filled my heart. The torch was only switched on once the riverbank obscured the horizon.

Shadow upon shadow, we slowly waded upstream – Mike, heron-like, probing the water with the thin beam of light. Suddenly, he stopped. There, in the watery glow, was a trout! Mike held the beam on the gently undulating fish. The trout seemed oblivious; almost serene - unaware of its close encounter with (and pending abduction by), aliens from another world.

Only when Mike scooped the fish from the stream with one swift movement of his net did it come to life. Well… briefly, at least.

Recently, I revisited the area and was saddened to learn of the death of Mike the previous season. Sorry to have missed him, I ventured out once more to the stream where he often said he felt most alive and where his ashes were now scattered. It was late in the day and, as the sun sank towards the horizon, both dusk and I crept slowly over the landscape.

A fish rose where years before we had poached.

Despite numerous casts, my fly was refused, until a sudden gust of wind caught my line and deposited the fly on the other side of the fish. Immediately, the trout took it!

After a short fight, I netted a young brownie. As I turned the fish over, I discovered the reason for the earlier refusals. The fish was blind in one eye!

I left the river with the uneasy feeling that for "Mike the Milk", his spirit and the trout, the karmic wheel had just turned…

It's Only Rock & Roll

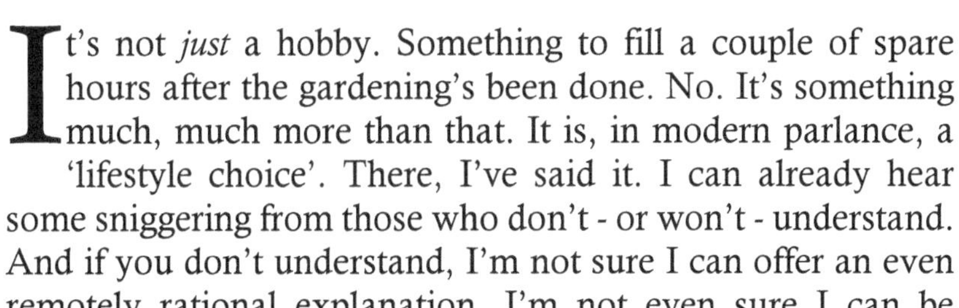

It's not *just* a hobby. Something to fill a couple of spare hours after the gardening's been done. No. It's something much, much more than that. It is, in modern parlance, a 'lifestyle choice'. There, I've said it. I can already hear some sniggering from those who don't - or won't - understand. And if you don't understand, I'm not sure I can offer an even remotely rational explanation. I'm not even sure I can be *bothered* trying to explain. You either get it or you don't and, in a strange and slightly selfish kind of way, I'm glad more people *don't* get it than do!

I am a fly fisherman, and it *is* a lifestyle choice. I love everything about it, including the way it has impacted on almost every aspect of my life. When I chose my college, I picked one surrounded by great fishing. I now live in a cottage with a trout river at the bottom of the garden. It goes without saying that I have a vast collection of fishing tackle and fly tying stuff; more than I could ever possibly use, even if I lived to be a centenarian. When I buy clothes, I consider how appropriate they are to wear while fishing. Like many, I also have an extensive library of fishing books, a lot of them yet to be read. I know I'm not alone in this obsession. I also have a guilty pleasure. A pleasure I generally do not share with others, for fear they really *will* think I do need psychiatric help. I love music. Folk, rock, pop, jazz, classical - all sorts. I know what you're thinking. *"Lots of people love music - even jazz! What's this guy's point?"* But that's not my secret. My secret is, I *love* fishing music! I know it sounds weird, but I'm certain it's not...

Let me explain. As I said, it's a lifestyle choice. When I can't go fishing, or read about it, or do a little fly-tying - especially when I'm in the car - I can listen to music. Fishing music. But what *is* fishing music? Well, most people of a certain age could probably name only one fishing song: *'Gone Fishin''* by Louis Armstrong and Bing Crosby - and while it is a great song, I would hate you to think I have it on a loop and listen to it endlessly. There is other stuff out there, and some of it is fantastic.

Music, much like fishing, can be incredibly powerful and emotionally affecting. It is capable of lifting your spirits in the same way certain aspects of nature can. It can trigger responses from deep in your soul, carrying you off to another place in your mind. A *better* place. And while there are many artists who fish (Eric Clapton and Steve Earle, for example), few of them are inspired to write or sing about fishing. Thankfully, however, there *are* some who appear just as obsessed as the rest of us! So if you're looking for some tracks to listen to on your drive to the water (or something to aid in carrying your spirit away from the reality of the moment to some mythical waterside idyll), let me 'count you down', in no particular order, my "Top Ten" – a piscine version of *"Top of the Pops"*, if you will…!

~ ~ ~

10. <u>Dusty Road To Beulah Land - Drew Nelson</u>
A great, earthy, rootsy collection of songs. New country, Americana… call it what you will. All these songs are from the heart, and it shows. Listen to *'Highway 2'*; all Drew needs is a trout stream. I know just how he feels.

9. <u>To Tulsa And Back - JJ Cale</u>
The late, great JJ Cale -- master of the laid-back, hypnotic, infectious groove. Any of his albums will put a smile on your face, and many feature Eric Clapton - a keen fly fisherman, as mentioned earlier (incidentally, listen to their classic album *'The Road To Escondido'*. It features a track called *'Ride The River'*, conjuring up images in my mind of floating one of the

great American rivers...) Track 5 on *'To Tulsa And Back'* is *'Stone River'*; a lament about the sorry state of a particular river, but which sadly applies to any number of rivers and streams across the continents…

8. <u>The River - Hamish Napier</u>

An entrancing album, mainly instrumental and very traditional in terms of instrumentation, yet at the same time quite contemporary in feel. The album is inspired by Hamish's love of the Spey, a river he grew up by, and features tracks such as *'The Mayfly'* and *'Spey Cast'*.

7. <u>Songs From Sun Street - The Saw Doctors</u>

Track 4: *'Carry Me Away'*. If ever a song was written for an angler to have playing at their funeral, this is it. Written by Carton and Moran (surely at least *one* of them must be an angler?!), this song evokes sad, wistful images of a peaceful Irish lough. It is full of nostalgic imagery of great times enjoyed, while acknowledging those times are, sadly, now gone forever…

6. <u>Rivers - Patrick Leonard</u>

Patrick Leonard is an American record producer and musician who has worked with the likes of Madonna, Rod Stewart, Bryan Ferry and Roger Waters - to name but a few. He is also a fly fisherman who happens to be a friend of John Gierach. This is a magnificent instrumental album, mainly piano based. The pieces are inspired by a nine-day fishing trip Leonard undertook in 1995. Gierach has contributed an introduction to the album, and it is gold dust. If you buy only *one* CD as a result of reading this, *'Rivers'* should be top of your list - although be warned; it is becoming increasingly difficult to find.

5. <u>Yellow Dog - Greg Brown</u>

A live CD with all the proceeds going to the Yellow Dog Watershed Preserve. Greg Brown is an American folk singer with a deep, resonant voice; sounding as though he's swallowed a skipful of gravel! He writes from the heart and his lyrics are witty, sad, joyous and suggestive… Suffice to say, he has all the bases covered. It's also worth seeking out his collaboration with the late Bill Morrissey on the *'Friend Of Mine'* album. Track 11, *'Fishing With Bill'*, feels like a more contemporary take on Armstrong and Crosby's duet on *'Gone Fishin''*.

4. <u>Slow Walking Water - Jazz & Fly Fishing</u>

A jazz quartet formed in Helsinki with a common love of jazz and fly fishing. The album is instrumental and inspired by time spent on the water. In addition to making great jazz, the four members are also purveyors of high-quality fishing films well-worth seeking out! Visit their website for more information: www.jazzandflyfishing.com

3. <u>Lead Me To The Water - Gary Brooker</u>

A great album featuring Eric Clapton and George Harrison, featuring three tracks inspired by the Procol Harum front man's love of fly fishing. One of the tracks, *'The Angler'*, was used many years ago by Peter Cockwill in a video he released on small-water trout fishing. A great album by an underrated musician.

2. <u>Catch And Release - Pete Clark & Gregor Lowery</u>

This duo hold a regular 'Troot Tour', combining live shows with great fishing locations and this album, consisting mainly of original instrumentals, is inspired by those trips. Two consummate traditional musicians, this CD is worth buying for track 10 alone; named after - and inspired by - the great Bruce Sandison!

1. <u>Anymore For Anymore - Ronnie Lane & Slim Chance</u>

A brilliant album that has stood the test of time. Originally released in '74, Lane nailed the 'Rustic Rock & Roll' vibe that many have tried, and failed, to fully capture. I think Ronnie *did* fish, he must have done! The stand-out track for me is *'The Poacher'*: "Bring me a fish with eyes of jewels and mirrors on its body...", every angler's mantra! While this is the only track on the album relating to fishing, the other songs - mostly original - gel to evoke a pastoral, rustic and sometimes rambunctious aural atmosphere to which I return again and again, either wishing I were fishing or out in the countryside, or when I just want to soundtrack a fly-tying session!

~ ~ ~

The above serves as small 'soundbites' of some of my favourite fishing music, as well as enthusiastic recommendations. There is lots more out there, though. You may find that discovering it, tracking it down and collecting it can, oftentimes, be almost as satisfying as stalking, hooking and landing a wild trout... *almost*.

It's only Rock 'n Roll, but I like it.

The Last Chance Fishing Club

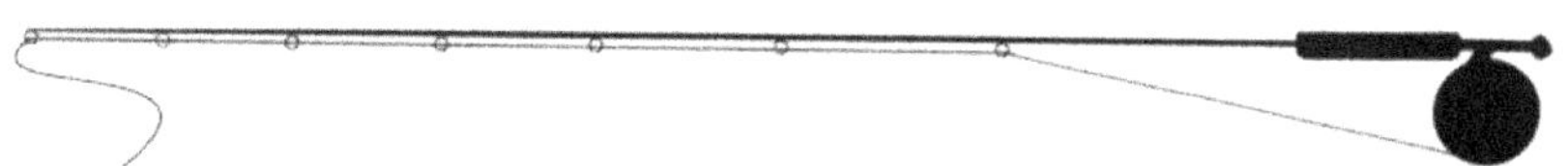

Sometimes, I think catching a fish is incidental to having a good time by the river. Then I have a blank day; realising it isn't. It would seem that while I'm not fooling the trout, I *am* fooling *myself.* But just one fish hooked - though not necessarily landed - will usually be sufficient to keep me content… at least for a while. Oftentimes, having caught that one fish, I will stop or at least take a break from fishing. *I need to.*

I need time to reflect on what has just happened; to contemplate the magical experience that has occurred, to be careful not to take it for granted. To be careful not to allow the experience to become devalued by unthinking repetition in a quest for instant gratification. I need time to just stand in the stream and feel the press of the water; the weight of life flowing around and through me. To feel the gravel begin to shift under my feet; pushed on by the relentless flow. To allow my gaze to follow the soft braid of currents downstream, to the point where it becomes impossible to differentiate between the surface of the water and the heavy, humid atmosphere. Where it becomes impossible to distinguish between the life coursing through my veins and the water pushing through the streams and rivers of my experience.

And all the time - all around - every life form you can imagine (and many that you can't), continue to be born; to grow, to reproduce and to die - all part of the great vortex that is nature. That great, indifferent vortex of shifting, flowing life to which you, as an individual, are of little - if any - consequence. We humans have a predilection for believing in our own importance; believing that *the world revolves around us.* It is an easy trap to fall into - and the more we fail to connect with nature, the more this dangerous, egocentric illusion will grow until - like all illusions - being exposed for the fatal lie that it is.

But something as ridiculous as trying to fool a fish with a fly can connect you to the real world. As the hook takes hold, you are hauled into the vortex. Above the surface, below the surface; the truth is all-pervading. In the gravel beneath your feet, life stirs - and is launched on an unstoppable journey which connects the molten core of the earth with the dancing corona of the sun.

All forms of life are connected and interdependent - and important, of course - yet only as a species. The individual exists only to make up the numbers. Yet, perversely, that is not the case with the trout with which I connect. Every single one is important to me. Important for where they take me. As the hook takes hold, the link is made. Not just in so much as my own life and the trout's, but the more critical connection; my artificial, sanitised, egocentric world connecting with the *real* world. A world of muscle, blood and bone; life and death, darkness and light, push and pull. A constant fight for survival. A life without regret and the weight of self-awareness to both hinder and deceive. A link is made. A connection with childhood; a connection with half-remembered dreams; a connection with a lost world. A connection with the *real* world...

High in the Berwyn mountains, the sparkling Ceiriog springs to life and begins its tumultuous race to the sea, via the Dee. Reputedly the fastest-flowing river in Wales, the Ceiriog runs roughly west to east. By the time it reaches the bottom of my garden - approximately half-way through its journey - it has matured into a delightful small stream, in most places no more than fifteen to twenty feet across, but still bright and sparkling as it forges its way down the Valley.

The Ceiriog Valley (known locally as the 'Valley of the Poets') is home to many writers and artists; strange, mysterious, almost reclusive characters who take inspiration from the area's lush landscape and rich mixture of history and myth. Many came to the Valley in the '60s when the area became a magnet for hippies and those seeking to establish a lifestyle based on the growing counter-culture movement.

From my back door, I often watch and listen as the pressing plait of currents pushes past the ancient Crogen battleground - where the invading English were defeated by the defending Welsh. The battleground is flanked by the river on one side, and by the *"Gate of the Dead"* on the other - an area set in ancient woodland featuring thousand-year-old oaks that reach skywards towards the dominating castle above. The river then tumbles away below a steeply wooded bank - featuring deep, foreboding caves - home to… well, who knows what…?

It is possible, on this border stream, to hook your trout in England and land it in Wales - having taken no more than a couple of steps during the playing. The wild trout are like quicksilver, and whether your weapon of choice is Tenkara or Tonkin; Graphite or Glass, they respond well to most methods of fly fishing, as long as you are stealthy in your approach. And this approach will pay dividends in other ways; the Valley is rich in wildlife, and the river attracts all manner of creature to its banks. Only last season, I stood transfixed as - in broad daylight - a young badger came down to drink from the cool waters. Its shimmering reflection danced with the dappled light under the dense canopy of trees before merging magically - almost imperceptibly - back into the undergrowth, the playful waters left undisturbed. The very same waters where I now stand, knee-deep, in the pulsing flow. Watching, listening and waiting. Silent and serene. Alert, yet relaxed. Conscious, yet dreamlike. And happy, yet sad. Aware of all that is so perfect, and of what could be lost in the blink of an eye. A perfection to which most seem to be blind. A perfection which, sometimes, even anglers themselves can unwittingly sabotage.

A few years ago, every evening on my way home from work, I would crawl along the bypass in an endless queue of traffic. I gradually became aware of a small, overgrown stream; barely visible beneath the tangle of vegetation that now engulfed and smothered it. Each evening, as I sat in the car, I would try to trace its course across the fields and beneath the road. Might it hold any trout? Could anything even survive in such a narrow and choked stream?

With hindsight, I should probably have left things there, but, being anxious to discover my own secret place potentially full of huge wild trout that nobody else knew about, I had to find out who owned the land and the fishing. As it turned out, this was relatively easily achieved. A few discreet enquiries pointed me in the direction of a local farmer, who obviously thought I was a complete idiot offering to pay him to fish what he regarded as a fishless, weed-choked ditch. But a deal was done on the strength of a handshake, and I now had exclusive access to about a mile and a half of my own private stretch of stream.

The initial visits seemed to confirm what the farmer had told me because I saw no sign of fish of any kind. In fact, the stream was so choked and overgrown that it was virtually impossible to cast a fly at any point, assuming you could fight your way through the undergrowth in the first place! A change of tactics was called for. Casting just wasn't an option, and there was no sign of fish rising on any of my visits. A new approach, therefore, was formulated in my mind. An approach which would have probably seen me banned from most other clubs - but since *this* club had only one member, and that member was me, *I* made the rules.

On my subsequent visit, I used a ten-foot rod and a short six-pound leader attached to a floating line. The long rod allowed me to poke the tip through the vegetation and lower a heavily weighted fly between the thick weed beds, which I then jigged up and down in what I hoped was an enticing manner. If I tell you that I had more two-pound plus wild brownies out of that stream in my first season than I had previously caught in my entire life, you will get the picture!

This happy arrangement continued for a couple of seasons. I would visit the water and, feeling content having caught a fish, would leave. What I didn't know was that I was being watched. When the farmer had asked how the fishing was, I confirmed that I had caught a few, but tried to be vague about the numbers and the size of the fish; you could say that I was... economical with the truth.

The farmer, however, was curious - and on various visits, had seen me catch some nice fish. The next time I went to pay him, he called me to one side and suggested the money I was paying him did not reflect the quality of the fishing. Of course, he was right. He thought that perhaps he should form a small syndicate of perhaps just half a dozen fishermen. What did I think of this potential plan? Naturally, not wanting to alienate him, I made all the right noises and reassured him that I had some close friends who I was sure would be interested. I would speak to them in confidence, and I was sure I could recruit enough of them to meet his financial demands without the need for him to go public.

And so, over the next couple of seasons, the arrangement was put on a more formal footing, and the syndicate became established. To be fair, we all continued to enjoy some exceptional fishing. But nothing in life stays the same and, under pressure from some syndicate members, the riverbank began to catch the attention of regular working parties - before too long it even became possible to cast a fly properly! Jungle warfare became a thing of the past, and I began to enjoy the fishing less and less.

As the seasons passed, the rent demands became ever greater, and a decision was taken to open the syndicate up to more members. The syndicate became a club, the banks became clearer (and manicured), and the fishing got tougher and tougher. Increased fishing pressure combined with bankside clearance changed the nature of the water and the fishing beyond all recognition. As the quality of the fishing declined, the membership began to fall - and the club was pressured by the members to carry out regular stocking.

For a while, the catch rates increased and the membership stabilised. However, the wild trout population began to dwindle and catches of the larger Browns that had occurred in the early days were now a thing of the past.

After a few seasons, it was becoming apparent that it was impossible to maintain a stable membership. The level of rent required to hold the fishing - combined with the cost of stockfish - meant that the membership was paying relatively high fees to fish a water that produced fewer and smaller fish than the local still waters.

Eventually, it became financially unviable to run the club, and several years ago the lease expired, all members going their separate ways.

A few weeks ago, I drove along the old bypass road again and looked for the stream, but it was no longer visible - having long been neglected. It is once again hidden beneath a tangle of bracken and weeds. That same evening, I returned with my rod, but *without* consent to fish. I crept towards the stream, forced my way through the undergrowth, and lowered my fly into the depths. I will leave it to your imagination as to what I hooked, if anything - but one thing is for certain: I will be leaving that particular stretch of water in peace.

We anglers have a duty to protect precious wild places, even if that sometimes means forsaking the chance of some exceptional fishing. Maybe angling should only be carried out where it is sustainable. If the ecology of the environment has to be compromised, then perhaps we should think twice before wading in. No stocking, catch and release, no wading in vulnerable places… I can live with all of these if, when I do fish, I can do so in an environment as wild and natural as possible. If we look after Mother Nature, she will look after us.

So let's recalibrate our expectations. When I was young and knew no better, I killed more wild fish than I should have, and I now regret that. I was, I think, trying to prove something. Happiness is a state of mind. We no longer need to fish for food, nor should we be fishing for kudos. Do we seriously believe it is right to populate our rivers with genetically modified, overweight trout in order to satisfy our lust for size and numbers? And all in the name of sport. Is this the world we really want?

Sometimes, just one or two wild fish, of a size appropriate for their environment, *should* be enough…

A Marginal Advantage

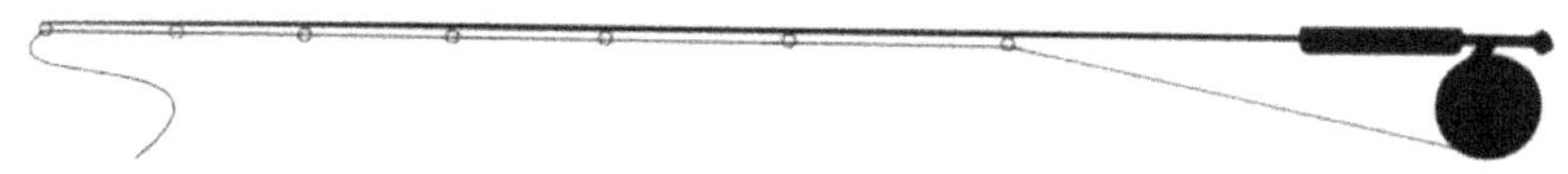

I think it was Neil Young who, when reflecting on the massive success of his album 'Harvest,' commented that while life in the middle of the road was very nice, life lived closer to the edge was much more interesting. Now, I don't know whether Mr. Young is a fly fisherman, but if not, he has inadvertently hit on one of the great truths in fishing. A truth it has taken me most of my fishing life to appreciate…

When you first start fly fishing, there seems to be so much detail to take in and learn, so many pieces of equipment required. But the biggest challenge of all is learning to cast. For me (and, I suspect, many others), this was quite a daunting challenge and in the sixties, when I first learned to fish, there were – unlike today - very few professional instructors and guides. And there was no way I could have even contemplated hiring one; pocket money didn't stretch that far, and even if I *could* have afforded the tuition, most of them seemed to be based in the south-east and focused mainly on chalk stream fishing. In any case, turning up at Farlows' with a solid glass fly rod wouldn't really have cut it.

But it seemed that casting was the thing; master the cast, and everything else would fall into place. And so began a journey where casting became the 'Holy Grail'. This was the period in which reservoir fishing boomed, so it seemed obvious that if you were facing an inland sea, the further you could chuck your fly, the better your chances of catching something! Every advertisement for rods and lines extolled their long-casting attributes. It was little wonder that some of us got sidetracked by all the hype.

I would be the first to agree that the ability to throw a long line can only be an advantage in your armoury. But what happened to me was that in my blinkered approach, I put my lack of success down to my inability to cast a full fly line, something which at the time seemed to be the absolute minimum required of a half-reasonable fly fisherman!

What got lost along the way was watercraft.

Unsurprising really, considering that watercraft is something you have to learn. There are no products marketed that will suddenly bestow upon you the powers of a trout-hunting God! Think about it…

We've all heard - and probably used at some point - the term, *"beginner's luck."* Picture the scene: a novice angler approaches the water and makes a tentative cast. The line barely goes beyond the rod tip, and the leader lands in a tangled heap. What happens next is enough to make any 'experienced' angler take up golf! The biggest fish to come out of the water in years takes the fly! Beginner's luck -- or is it…?

Watch any really good angler and he will approach the water with caution, exploring the margins of the river or lake, because he knows that fish love to live life close to the edge. The margins offer food and shelter, and where there is food and shelter is where you will find most of Earth's creatures – ourselves included. What our novice had unwittingly done was to place his fly exactly where there was a good chance of finding a fish. Secondly (particularly if he was fishing moving water), he had cast so badly that his leader had failed to straighten out - thus causing drag - making the fly behave unnaturally and putting off any self-respecting fish!

Since "seeing the light", I have begun catching a lot more fish. I now regard casting as far as I can towards the horizon or far bank as a last resort, and rarely catch much. Even when fishing in the sea, the approach is the same. I've caught bass in water less than knee-deep, and have often waded out beyond the fish, eventually landing them by turning around and casting back towards the shore. The same with mullet. On one of the most successful trips I had, I was sitting at the waters' edge with the waves lapping around my waist, casting a few feet into a shoal of fish exploring the tideline.

So if like me your casting leaves a lot to be desired, don't despair! *Embrace* your weaknesses, and you may find they eventually transform into your strengths. Live your fishing life closer to the edge - it really will give you a marginal advantage.

The Doghouse Trout

I feel unfettered and alive. The river - like the day - rolls out before me; its surface dimpled with endless possibilities. The bank-side grasses, thigh-high in the warming morning breeze, fill my senses with a heady mix of sound and scent.

To my right is a lichen-covered drovers bridge built from stones as old as time itself. Four or five feet above the water's surface is a small crevice in the stonework which has been home to a pair of dippers for as long as I have fished here, and no doubt much longer. To my left, a twisting track leads up to the castle. Ahead of me is the constant, liquid pewter river; tempting me, full of mystery and promise, compelling me deep into the press of it's cool, soothing waters.

"Be home by four o'clock at the latest!" are my orders; there is an 'important do' to attend, and my presence is required. Apparently, this is not up for negotiation. Family can be very demanding, particularly so for the obsessive flyfisherman. Still, I have a few hours ahcad of me as a free man...

I wander slowly upstream, scanning the surface for signs of activity. It is early spring, and the air is filled with birdsong. New growth is all-pervading, and there is a comforting, gentle warmth about the day. It feels good to be alive. There are insects everywhere - including on the surface of the water - but as of yet, no rises. It is a rise that I need to see. I can't effectively articulate the reasons why, but I usually only now fish a dry fly because it makes me happy; nothing more, nothing less. I no longer *have* to catch a fish, but I won't pretend that it's still not a significant event for me, and one that I like to repeat whenever possible. But it needs to be on *my* terms. It seems that it's just not as *vital* as it once was... Whether that's a good thing or not - or even the truth - I've yet to decide.

My slow meander upstream is a chance to relax, unwind and observe. I pause occasionally, trying to differentiate between fronds of waving weed beneath the distorting, sparkling surface and what I hope is a feeding trout. Seldom is it ever a feeding trout.

Halfway down the Crogen field is a fallen oak tree which, until the recent storms, stood tall and proud and provided a useful landmark. Now, in a final act of defiance, the centuries-old trunk straddles the river, forming a rustic, twisted bridge. One of its substantial limbs has dug into the riverbed and deflected the water hard into the far bank, scouring out a decent pool. So far this season, I have failed to catch anything from here, despite it looking to be a perfect spot.

I sit for a while - shielded from the river by the tree, but still able to see the surface of the pool through the maze of sun-bleached, brittle branches.

Upon first fishing this river, it was something of a puzzle to me. Although I had fished for years since childhood, it proved to be a real challenge. Up until then, I had fished many different types of water, from benign chalk streams to the restless rivers of the Yorkshire Dales, and I had caught enough trout to keep me content, but still interested. This river was tough. It flows down a luscious, verdant, steep-sided valley; rich in myth, folklore and abundant flora and fauna. But the gradient is severe - and as a result, the speed of the flow is formidable. There are few traditional holding pools, and at times you can be convinced that the river is just one long, barrelling riffle. No sooner has your fly alighted on the surface than it has been swept away below you in a matter of seconds. For a dry fly addict like me, this can prove problematic. However, as always, a little perseverance combined with a streak of stubbornness began to pay dividends.

For a while, I fished nymphs and wet flies (and sometimes Tenkara), which was fun. But still, I yearned to catch the small quicksilver trout on a floating fly – preferably my favourite, a

Yellow Humpy - gently cast using my pretty split cane rod, another favoured piece of equipment. By adopting a technique of short-range casts with a relatively short leader, I gradually discovered that the trout *could* be caught, but only if my reactions matched the lightning speed of the trout's sudden ambush of the fly. If not, I was left with just an explosion of spray and a drowned fly. Later on, I learned that this was a classic pocket water style of fishing, known and practised by many but not, until then, by myself. On this river, the pockets were small; so usually were the trout, and I had to learn the hard way. But the rewards, though sparse, were appreciated. Even though it was a challenge, it was a good lesson to learn. An important one too; because sometimes we can get a little complacent. Sometimes it's easy to assume that we're better fishermen than the reality would suggest - especially if we restrict ourselves to only our home rivers.

As I watch the pool, I become aware. *Very* aware. Of what, I'm not quite sure, but something has suddenly caused my senses to 'switch on'. I freeze. My hackles rise. My breathing slows, and I stare hard beneath the surface. For a moment, time seems to stand still. Nothing exists outside of my immediate focus. Something is about to happen. That fisherman's "sixth sense" kicks in suddenly to overdrive. Then my circuitry explodes! My pulse quickens. My hands tremble. There, just beneath the surface, is a trout. It's larger than any I have seen before on this particular river and, indeed, most of the rivers I have ever fished before. Save for my trembling hands, I'm motionless. Save for its imperceptibly quivering fins, so is the fish.

Minutes pass - the trout and I seemingly locked in a kind of limbo. The fish unaware, and me transfixed; unable and unwilling to move for fear of revealing my presence. I feel as if I am drifting into an almost trance-like state. My vision tricks me into believing that the fish is drifting too, in and out of my sight. I blink hard, and there it is again - every scale as clear as day, winking at me from below the surface. I blink again. This time the trout does not reappear. I blink a third time, then yet again - then several times in rapid succession in the vain hope that as my focus sharpens the fish will somehow reappear as if by magic. It doesn't. I slowly rise to my feet, frantically scanning the water. Nothing. I sit for a while, hoping that the fish will reappear. After about twenty minutes or so, I decide to move on. I'll explore further upstream for the rest of the afternoon, I decide. I know I'll have to pass the pool again on my way home. Perhaps by then, the fish will be back in residence.

For the remainder of the day, I wander upriver; casting occasionally, and even hooking a couple of small wild brownies - fish that normally I would be delighted to have caught. Today, however, I feel distracted. I don't fish well. If I am honest, I don't feel that I deserve the couple of fish that I've had. My mind has been elsewhere. The image of the big fish has haunted my every waking moment of the day. I turn around and head back to the pool. The grass is still flattened where previously I had staked out its lie. I make an exaggerated loop away from the bank in order to conceal myself, before taking up position again by the fallen oak tree. The afternoon is beginning to warm up now, and as I lean against a tree root, I feel my eyelids begin to close...

I awake with a start. The day's heat has dissipated. My back aches, and I feel chilly. I slowly raise myself to my knees and peer hard into the river. It takes my eyes a little time to adjust to the awkward light. After a few moments, I start to imagine that I can make out a huge tail fin, gently undulating beneath the surface. I squint, contorting my brow in the belief that it will improve my vision. It does. My heart pounds as the whole of the fish gradually materialises - in crystal clarity - right before my eyes. From the blue smear on its gill plate to the creamy white edging on its huge fins, it's a magnificent specimen!

Despite my knees starting to cramp, I dare not move. Suddenly, the fish tips up and takes something from the surface. A few seconds later, it does it again. I realise that this is the fish of a lifetime, and I know that I will have only one shot - no mistakes, no excuses. In exaggerated slow motion, I manoeuvre myself into position. I still have the Humpy on my leader, and although I am sure it is unlike any insect that any self-respecting fish on this river has ever seen, I decide to keep it on. I fear that in the time it takes me to change flies, the fish may well have disappeared. And what would I put in place of the Humpy? I have no idea what the fish has been feeding on and, as there is no visible hatch, I'll stick with it. Still on my knees, I shuffle into position. I pull off a few feet of line from my reel and check all around me to make sure that there is nothing to foul the coils on the ground. I slowly start to raise the rod tip, proceeding to accelerate the movement just sufficiently to propel the line behind me. It clears the barbed wire fence before pausing briefly, then, flicking the tip forward, I aim the fly about five feet ahead of where I judge the fish to be.

Time again stands still. In stuttering freeze-frames, the water beneath the fly lifts before settling. A large yellowish-brown neb cautiously nudges the fly. The Humpy settles again. Then, it's gone. As I struggle to my feet, I lift the rod tip and feel a satisfying weight. The little rod hoops over in response to the bulk of the fish and line peels off the reel. Thankfully, the fish stays within the pool. After a number of heart-stopping moments fuelled by growing self-doubt, I eventually slide the fish over the rim of my net. I don't lift the net from the water for fear that it will buckle and damage the fish. As I admire the magnificent creature, I struggle to recall a time when I have ever felt so happy and alive. I don't photograph the trout, as I have left my phone at home. I won't 'guesstimate' its size, but it's more than big enough for me. I gently remove the hook, facing the fish into the current, and, after a few seconds, let it kick away into the flow.

~

For a few minutes, I sit on the fallen trunk and just savour the moment; I don't want my euphoria to ebb. But ebb it does when I check my watch; 5:17 pm! Damn! I have lost all track of time, and now I'm late. I quickly gather all my tackle together and make for home. As I cross the fields, the cottage comes into sight. There is no sign of life. This is not looking good. If only I hadn't forgotten my phone. I gingerly approach the back porch. Still no signs of life.

As I enter the kitchen, something catches my eye. A note. It's been attached to the fridge, held in place by a 'cross face emoji' magnet. In angry red biro, it reads:

WELCOME TO THE DOGHOUSE!!

My heart sinks. How could I have been so selfish? What had been a great day has been ruined by my thoughtless behaviour. I've let the rest of the family down. I put my tackle on the kitchen island, and just as I am about to start cleaning it, the door into the dining room opens and in walks Lesley, a broad grin on her face. "Aren't you the lucky one?" she says.

Does she mean the fish? How could she know?

"Just after you left" she continued, "I had a call to say the party was cancelled. Vickie isn't feeling too good, so maybe we'll meet next week instead. I tried to call you, but you'd left your mobile in the lounge."

I smile weakly, and before I can concoct a reason to justify my thoughtlessness, she asks me with a twinkle in her eye, "Did you like my note?"

It would appear, much like the trout, I too had been let off the hook...

Anglerholics Anonymous

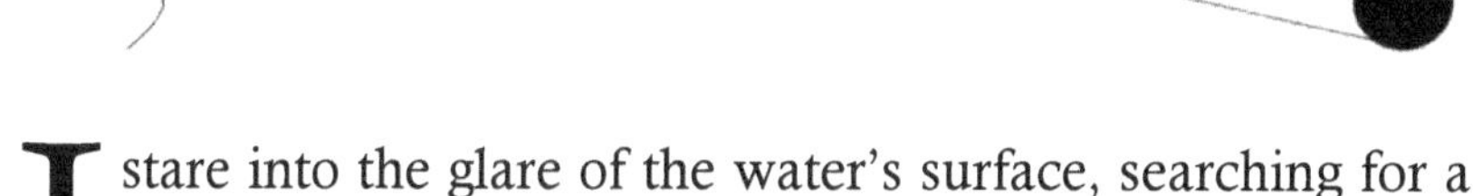

I stare into the glare of the water's surface, searching for a sign. Just *one more cast*. I should've been back over an hour ago - but here is a chance to save the day. Just one more *'last cast.'* This one really *will* be the last! I wait, and watch...

It seems the world has closed in on me. Nothing exists outside this egocentric bubble I have created. It's just me, and the trout... All my senses are tuned in to pinpointing the lie of the fish. I know I'll have only one shot at this. I slowly remove the fly from the keeper ring and blow on it. There! A rise. And another! I carefully draw line from the reel, aerialise what I judge to be just enough, and let the cast go. Time seems to stand still. Just let me hook this *one* fish, please. Then I'll go... just *one fish*, that's all I want - that's all I *need... **please!***

The unrelenting craving to feed this addiction began when I was still at school. The River Clwyd was just a short bike-ride from home, and for a few years I would fish two or three days a week following the school-day's merciful end. If a week went by without catching a trout, I would automatically believe I was losing my touch; unworthy of calling myself a fisherman. It was a temporary infatuation, family and friends assumed, that I would surely grow out of sooner rather than later. But my obsession was growing insidiously into addiction... slowly spiraling out of control... and no one could possibly have suspected or seen it coming.

The fly alights gently on the water's surface, about twelve inches upstream of the trout's last rise. My world has slowed to a series of silent, stuttering freeze-frames as the fly drifts its way toward the fish. Breathing is involuntarily suspended as an uncontrollable trembling telegraphs my anxiety down the line and into the river. Please, please, *please* take the fly - I promise I will let you go and then pack up! *I promise!*

The outcome, as I already know in my heart-of-hearts, is academic. Like all addicts, I will return again and again; making the same promises, saying the same selfish prayers and never really wanting to be free of my obsession.
My name is Steven Murgatroyd, and I am an anglerholic.

I'm alone now in a small, sparsely furnished room; typical of the kind every hospital in the country must have. No windows: just a bed and a chair in the corner; "Property of Psychiatric Dept." hand-painted in bold red lettering on its scratched and pitted wooden back.

The door opens. "*Ah!* Mr. Murgatroyd, my name is Dr. Sandison." A pristinely white-coated figure looms in front of me. He appears slightly distracted as he reads through the notes on his clipboard. "I understand you have been referred to me by your GP. He tells me that he and your family have become increasingly concerned as to your behaviour lately. Do get up on the bed. Now, perhaps you would like to tell me all about it?"

I explain how my obsession has manifested over the years. The sprawling library of fishing books and magazines; the crockery and the clothes, the cufflinks… even the wristwatches featuring angling motifs! Then there are the piscatorial paintings and photographs in just about every room in the house, the CDs, the DVDs (even the odd dusty, obsolete VHS tape!), the holidays and the courses, the fly-tying equipment and all the hobby entails, and now - the environmental politics… !

"*Stop! Stop!*" cries Dr. Sandison. "What I need you to explain to me is *why?*'

"Well," I continue, "I think my love of fishing is fuelled by the fact it allows me to connect with the natural world -- recapture elements of simpler times when life, the world and everything in it wasn't so complicated." I pause, throwing a glance the doctor's way. He nods, encouraging me to continue.

"I suppose I just want to protect my fishing and everything it means to me. Not just for selfish reasons - though I admit that is probably a big part of it – but also to help safeguard the environment from the myriad threats increasing on a daily basis..."

Dr. Sandison stops taking notes, pulls up the chair and sits down. He motions me to elaborate.

"Look," I press on, "if by supporting a business that donates money to conservation helps to protect the environment — even if it means I end up with a house full of stuff sporting fish motifs — then I will. Every conservation body aiming to protect what I love will also get my support." I am now well into my stride. "I just think it's kind of embarrassing that some of us are regarded as slightly odd when we find ourselves fighting to protect things you would have thought society's collective common sense would automatically value and strive to protect. Things like fighting water abstraction and pollution, not allowing development and mining in inappropriate locations, or the siting of fish farms where damage to wild fish stocks is inevitable! Not to mention- -"

"Mr. Murgatroyd," the doctor interrupts, "I think I've heard enough to enable me to give you my initial diagnosis."

Dr. Sandison rises to his feet, studying the cracks on the ceiling as he continues. "I have both good news and bad news. Firstly, the good. I personally believe that you and others like you are perfectly sane! The bad news is everybody *else* is mad; the lunatics really have taken over the asylum!" With a smile, he opens the door to usher me out. "Don't give up the fight!"

As I turn to shake his hand, I notice the image of a leaping trout embroidered on his tie.

"A Whiter Shade of Pale Watery Dun"

An interview with Procol Harum's Gary Brooker

It is 1967. The summer of love, flower power and Sgt. Pepper. The Beatles are at their creative peak, and the world - at least through my young eyes - appears to be a kaleidoscope of colour and sound. I am about to start secondary school. Everything is new, anything is possible, and life seems exciting and frightening in equal measure. There is one particular song that can take me back to those times as if they were yesterday.

'A Whiter Shade of Pale', Procol Harum's huge world-wide hit, plays a major part in the soundtrack of the sixties. Selling somewhere between six and ten million copies, depending on whose figures you believe, the song is the most played record by British broadcasters and the most played record in public places. It is a classic anthem of its time and one of the biggest-selling singles ever.

Fast-forward fifty years. I am sitting in the weak spring sunshine with one of the song's co-writers and the band's frontman, Gary Brooker. I can't help thinking to myself how strange life can be; to find myself opposite a man who I used to watch on *'Top of the Pops'* and who, due to a shared passion for fly fishing, I am now conversing with.

I asked Gary how long he has fished. He told me; "I was about five years of age and, like most youngsters, I was fascinated by water. We used to play down by the local river, and it was a natural progression to try to catch the magical creatures that hid in the deep, dark, mysterious depths. My first fish was a minnow, and I was hooked for life". Gary firmly believes that angling for sport is a modern manifestation of a long-suppressed hunting gene. Born in 1945, Gary pursued his love of angling all through his formative years, but music soon began to compete for his spare time. He would, however, continue to fish whenever possible. It was in the early seventies that Gary was introduced to fly fishing. His devotion to the sport has remained ever since; resulting in many trips, both in the U.K. and abroad, in search of a wide variety of species.

In Gary's own words, at one point he "went a bit mad", and became almost obsessed with the sport to the extent that he was doing little else besides fishing, along with building his own rods, inventing tools to make the process easier and amassing a vast collection of fly-tying materials - many of which would be impossible to source these days, due to changes in legislation. (You will be relieved to learn that I resisted asking Gary if he has managed to tie a whiter shade of Pale Watery Dun!)

This period of Gary's life also saw him venture into the tackle trade. While competing in a fly-casting competition at a local country fair, Gary met Peter Cockwill - the well-known fishing guide and writer. Their friendship developed, resulting in the two of them opening a tackle shop together. Eventually, Peter went solo with the project and still runs a very successful fly fishing shop in Surrey. This shop, however, was not their only joint venture. Gary, along with renowned fly tier Taff Price, played a major role in the production of a video entitled *'Fly Fishing in Clear Waters'*. Gary not only featured in the film but also produced, directed, and composed the soundtrack. The main musical theme of the film is from a track on Gary's 1982 album *'Lead Me to the Water'*, titled *'The Angler'*. The album features several tracks inspired by Gary's love of fly fishing and features appearances by Eric Clapton, George Harrison and Phil Collins. Gary is also responsible for introducing Clapton to fly fishing - a sport that he, too, is now passionate about.

Interestingly, the back cover of the album sleeve features a photograph of Gary snoozing on the porch of a cabin by the Deschutes in Oregon - having at last caught, after several days of trying, a good-sized steelhead. This event inspired the aforementioned *'The Angler'* and, as we sat talking, Gary recited an excerpt from the lyrics to me…

> *'But on the thirteenth morning when the sun was high*
> *He tricked that steelhead and saw the line go tight*
> *Two spirits fighting Two creatures bold*
> *Bad luck and trouble had finally lost their hold'*

A magical moment. The album cover also carries a paraphrase of a quote from *'The Compleat Angler'* - Walton being his favourite angling writer.

I asked Gary about his current approach to fishing, and he told me that he still has a real passion for fly-tying. A creation of Gary's called the *'Martinez'* features in the book, *'The World Fly Finder'* by Peter Cockwill. Over the years, Gary has gathered an extensive collection of fishing books and tackle - in particular, a large number of cane fly rods. He has a penchant for Hardy tackle, and his trusty Hardy Smuggler often accompanies him when on the road. If good fishing lies near a concert venue, then Gary will often set aside some time to go fishing.

Although his approach to fishing today is perhaps not as intensive as it once was, Gary still fishes with the same passion as he did in his younger days. He smiles as he recalls an episode in the late eighties when he ended up being presented with a medal in the European Open Championship: "I accompanied the team abroad. I think they only wanted me because I can speak fluent French and was handy on the 'ivories' for a sing-song in the evening! However, one member of the team was taken ill, and I was asked to step in at the last minute and, would you believe it, I had a really good session and ended up with a medal!"

Gary acknowledges that he is in the lucky position of often being given the chance to fish on some of the most prestigious rivers in the country with some very famous musician friends. He tells me that he believes that musicians have an advantage over many when it comes to casting, as they instinctively have good timing and find it no problem to pause on the backcast. He also believes in the therapeutic aspect of the sport in so much as when you are fly fishing, you tend to live very much 'in the moment' - concentrating on the complexities of casting, currents, rise forms and fly-grabbing vegetation!

Just as 1967 was a life-changing year for Gary, so too was 2017. It is now over fifty years since *'A Whiter Shade of Pale'* hit the charts, and at the time of writing, Gary and Procol Harum are about to hit the road again to promote their new album, *'Novum'*. Let's hope that at least a couple of the venues have some fishing close by!

Lyrics to 'The Angler', Copyright © Bluebeard/Rondor Music.

Tying instructions for the Martinez - Gary's general-purpose still water nymph pattern:

Hook : 8 to 12 standard shank or 2x nymph
Tail : A few fibres of Guinea Fowl feather
Body : Black Rabbit underfur dubbed and ribbed with silver wire
Thorax : Black Rabbit underfur with a green raffine wing case over
Hackle : Two turns of grey partridge

A wonderfully buggy fly that fishes all year round, but is best in spring and early summer!
Source: World Fly Finder by Peter Cockwill

Tattoos and Battle Scars

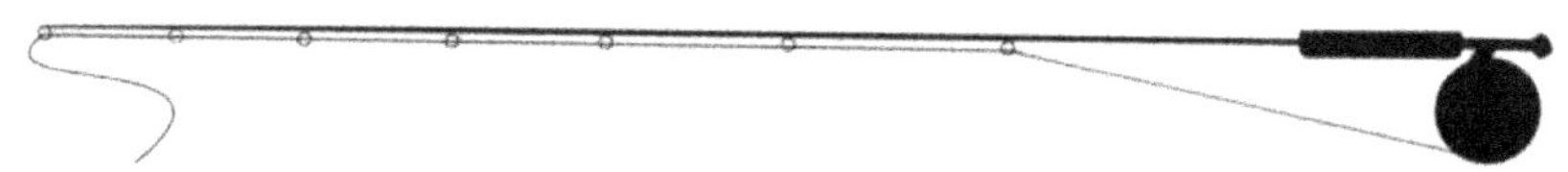

This was a fish that tattooed its image into your brain.

The Hardy Jet bowed in deference as the fish turned its flank to the current to form a living, shimmering dam. Then; an explosion of power - a leap - projecting a cascade of sunlit droplets, arching high into the air, before letting the stream carry it and my fly away, forever...

I do have other tattoos; all etched deeply within my psyche - indelible images still burning bright with the sweet sorrow of the loss of something you dared only dream about - but could never possess. The opiate of the fisherman. But this was my first; a virtual slow-motion film, to be replayed at will, never fading and archived deep within my memory - an instant fix detailed in a sequence of freeze-frames.

Wilbury also has tattoos. None of them (at least, not the ones he flaunts) have anything to do with fishing, particularly the one he claims as his first - a relic of his days spent around the Gulf Coast in the early 70s. He'll say no more than that. The image, he says, speaks for itself. Being a man of few words is something Wilbury nurtures - although you would never hear him admit to it!

"Better to be silent and thought a fool, than to speak and be proved one," says Wilbury - which I take as my cue to cut the chatter.

We've been aboard 'Moonriser' for several hours now. Virtually becalmed, our thoughts and idle musings have spanned the years and bridged the continents while we, as if tethered by an invisible anchor line, have barely moved. I am now starting to present with the early signs of sunstroke, dehydration and lack of fish. I'm red in the face, irritable and frustrated. Wilbury dozes in the bow. We'd travelled north to the big lochs in search of pike, keen to extend our tally of "legitimate" fly-caught fish. I say legitimate, as I have caught pike whilst trout fishing and vice versa - but sometimes it is nice to accomplish what you set out to achieve.

I've always been dogged by irony in my fly fishing. Unintentionally, I have caught fish on sunken dries and some on floating wets. I've caught fish when using floating lines that refused to float, and some on sinking lines that wouldn't. I have even had fish take bare hooks and strike indicators.

None of this enhances my credibility.

Wilbury says I take it all too seriously; catching a fish is catching a fish! Relax, enjoy it! `Moonriser' is becalmed. We start to drift in and out of consciousness. As the sun rises higher, we doze deeper and relive memories of previous expeditions, temporarily oblivious to the realities of the world around us.

It's the cool breeze on my face and the sound of waves slapping at the hull that rouses me from my daydreams. It's now early evening, and the weather has turned. A fresh breeze from the west has pushed us toward Rabbit Island.

Dark clouds crowd the sky, and white horses start across the lake. As the Dog Star rages and hounds the sun from the sky, we abandon any thoughts of rowing back across the water to the sanctuary of the boathouse and decide to land on the island. If necessary, we can tough out the storm and sleep beneath the upturned boat.

Having beached the boat, Willbury suggests that we should seek out the lee shore and try to catch something so we can eat.

He hooks a pike on the first cast. As it tail-walks across the waves, the hook pulls out! The fish looked to be about 101b. I flog away, struggling to get the fly much beyond the rod tip as the wind quarters around. Just as I am about to lift the fly from the water for another attempt, a small perch takes it.

Wilbury starts to build a fire.

"Put a trout fly on," he tells me. "And see if you can catch something worth eating!"

In the twilight, I search through my fly-box, grasping a Soldier Palmer as the wind tries to snatch it away from me. Foolishly, I congratulate myself on my small victory over the elements. Now, squinting in the gloom, I somehow manage to tie the fly to my leader and, on my first cast, I catch a small perch!

As Wilbury cleans the fish, I attempt one last cast. The winds of revenge are now blowing. Snatching the Soldier Palmer on the back-cast, the wind mercilessly pummels it - and the fly line – directly into the back of my neck!

Wilbury, with all the dexterity of an abattoir apprentice, eventually extracts the hook from my bleeding, stinging flesh.

"Just a small cut!" he beams, almost gleefully. "Think of it as a battle scar - a tattoo to remind you of this adventure. What fly was it? A Soldier Palmer? There you are! Think of it as a Military Tattoo!"

Sometimes… just sometimes… fishing with Wilbury is a real pain in the neck!

Fly Rods, Whisky and Wild, Wild Trout

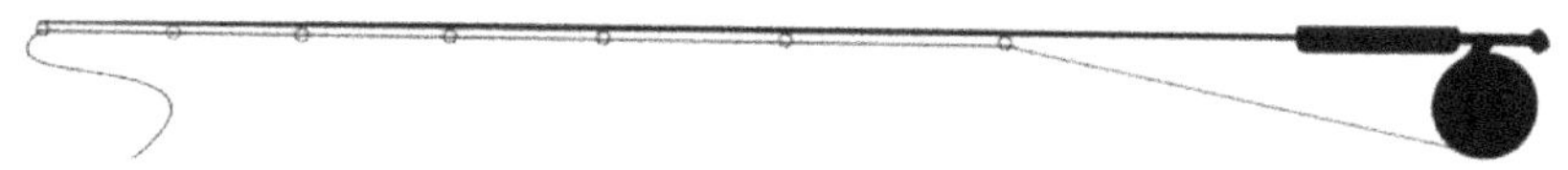

"Kaleela! *Kaleeeela!*" Mario's victorious battle-cry boomed along the beach, signifying he was into a fish. Paul and I looked on as Mario backed up the shingle beach to land the Sea Trout. "Kaleela!" we responded, acknowledging, with a slight tinge of envy that this was a pretty special moment and something we all wanted to achieve. Although catching Sea Trout from the shore was not the primary reason for our visit to Islay, it can be a realistic option. Admittedly, hitting that perfect combination of tides, weather, location and fickle feeding fish is something of a lottery; but, as Mario had just proved; it *is* possible. Although that was the only fish between the three of us that evening, it demonstrated the possibilities the Island presents the visiting angler.

From my home in the Welsh marches, the drive takes several hours to the ferry port of Kennacraig on Scotland's West Coast. It's a fairly easy journey. Motorway, for the most part, continuing on to single carriageway roads set against a magnificent backdrop of hills and lochs on a grand scale - - some of the most spectacular scenery the United Kingdom has to offer.

I met up with Mario at the ferry terminal car park, and we spent the next couple of hours (the time it takes to make the crossing to Islay, incidentally!) chatting about our hopes for the coming week. Things were looking good! Paul, the third member of our party who had travelled to the Island ahead of us, posted a photo on Mario's social media feed of himself with a pretty, wild trout having been caught within a couple of hours of arriving. As we sailed past the inviting "Paps of Jura", expectations were running as high as you dare let them on a trip to unfamiliar waters.

Islay (pronounced *'Eyela'*) is the southernmost of the Inner Hebrides islands, off the West Coast of Scotland. Along with the neighbouring Island of Jura, it's particularly well known for its whisky, fishing, birdwatching and historical interest. Numerous distilleries produce the Island's characteristically peaty single malts. In the north-east, two islands on Loch Finlaggan are dotted with the remains of an ancient settlement, including a prehistoric fort and medieval tombstones. The loch also boasts areas of deep, gripping peat bogs - more on that later...!

~

We were to spend the week staying with our host David Wood, in a charming, comfortable, well-proportioned white-rendered house on the banks of Loch Skerrols. David is not only a knowledgeable and experienced angler, but, having spent most of his career in the industry, is also something of a whisky connoisseur. In addition, he runs 'Fly Fish Islay,' the guiding service I booked with. Not a bad way to earn a living (although I suspect it is not the "walk in park" those of us who work nine-to-five may, with a touch of envy, like to believe it is). Could things get any better? Well, the weather - for most of the week - was kind; clear blue skies and warm sunshine. This, combined with a reasonable breeze, gave us near-perfect fishing conditions! On a number of days, we even had to cover up to protect against sunburn! We visited in May, and despite being forewarned about wild weather and midges the trip was, for the most part, exactly what you would have wished for.

This was my first foray into Scottish loch fishing, although I had previously fished a few Welsh Llyns and so, aware of how much precious fishing time one can waste trying to find and access the waters when visiting a new location alone, I opted to join an organised, guided trip. By the end of the week, I was convinced it had been money well spent.

Although an itinerary had been produced beforehand, it was by no means set in stone, and plans for the following days fishing were always discussed around the dinner table the evening prior. David was very open to changing the schedule to accommodate the group's preferences and aspirations. I think I would be right in saying the three of us really wanted to experience true wild trout fishing in remote wilderness locations and this is exactly what was provided. Of course, there is often a price to be paid in order to achieve this, in the form of strenuous uphill walks and yomping over gloopy peat bogs. When you finally crest that final summit, however, and see a sparkling loch below you replete with the rings of rising trout, you know it's all been worthwhile, aching legs and breathlessness soon forgotten.

But not *all* the fishing involved a hike - a number of lochs we fished were very easily accessible by car, and the fishing was excellent. The quality of the fish we caught was a surprise. I think we all expected to catch rather thin, dark fish; fish that survived rather than thrived, and while we did catch a few of that ilk, we also caught a good number of very pretty, plump fish; testament to the quality of the habitat.

The trip proved to be a true holiday; you could, if you wished, fish from sunrise to sunset. Alternatively, if you wanted to fish for just a couple of hours and go off and visit one of the Islands distilleries, that was no problem either. This flexibility makes for a very enjoyable experience even if, like me, you tend to be a bit of a loner with regard to your fishing, having somewhat of an aversion to group activities in general…

At the end of each day, all our wet gear went into the drying room and we retired, dram in hand, to the splendid sitting room; with its views over Loch Skerrols, to recount the day's activities and await David's latest culinary masterpiece to emerge from the kitchen. The food (some might call it 'man food'), was excellent. Tasty, well-cooked, in more-than-sufficient quantity. And, thankfully, not a salad in sight; so no need to feel guilt for going with the tasty option!

In terms of gear, I fished most of the time with 9'6" to 10' rods, 5 to 7 weight - the heavier rods coming out only if the wind dictated. Traditional loch flies covered most situations, although at one point Paul did resort to 'klink and dink' techniques to fool some particularly fussy fish.

We fished from the bank all week, and never did it limit our enjoyment or catch rate. Chest waders were the order of the day (not because deep wading was required; most of the lochs have extensive shallows which appear to hold plenty of fish), but rather as protection from adders, sunburn and ticks. Luckily, serious encounters with all three were avoided.

The lochs we fished, which included Giur-bheinn, Drolsay, Finlaggan, Nan Cadhan and Skerrols, ranged in size from a few acres to much more substantial bodies of water, but even the larger lochs could be circumnavigated by foot during the course of a day's fishing. Despite my somewhat solitary tendencies, I would strongly recommend fishing with -- or at least being within shouting distance of -- another angler. Finlaggan almost claimed my scalp when, in an attempt to take a shortcut across what turned out to be a deep peat bog, I sank up to my knees. Eventually I managed to extricate myself, but it's not too difficult to imagine a less satisfactory outcome, like something out of an old E.C. horror comic.

As with all great trips, time flew and the week was soon over. After a great lunch at one of the Island's distilleries, it was time to board the ferry for the return trip. I realised that during the whole week I had managed to avoid television, radio and newspapers, but had seen my first White Tailed Sea Eagle, first Choughs and first Adder... not a bad trade-off! As we sailed once again past the Paps of Jura, it also dawned on me that I hadn't spoken with a woman since I arrived...! It was, I decided, definitely time to go home and plan the next trip.

(Oh, in case you're wondering - - 'Kaleela', Mario's battle-cry, was based on the name of his favourite Islay whisky; Caol Ila.)

Genesis

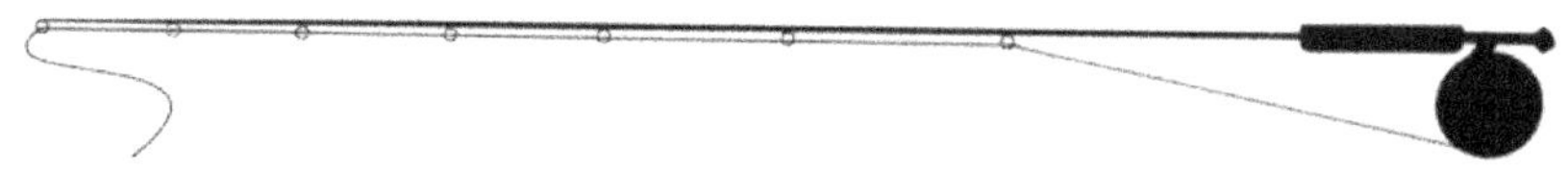

Some say fishing ruined me. I say fishing made me...

The fish was big. I was small. It did what only fish can do; without any obvious movement, it began a slow-motion fade. It took me a moment to realise, empty-headed, I was staring at empty water. Could I really have seen such a beautiful thing? Or was it just a daydream - a trick of the light, a flick of the tail? Now, at sixty-something, I can still see that watery jewel. Teasing me, tempting me... just as it did on that sixties' summer's day when, net in hand, a tadpole hunter became a fisherman.

You would be forgiven for assuming, given I'm a fanatical Flyfisher, that the fish in question was a trout. It was not. It was a carp. Bronze, fully scaled, a strong head, broad fins and a muscular, tapered body.

Fast-forward half a century, and once again I am bankside. I am still doing what all fishermen do: staring intently into the depths. Searching for a sign; for movement, for anything to validate my obsession...

The pool is small, hidden in a gentle fold in the countryside. There are two benign inlets which supply and refresh the pool before the water exits at the southern end into a hidden culvert. The southern end is shallower and more open, sporting good weed growth. Perfect cover in which a fish can bask in safety. But I am halfway down the more heavily wooded bank where the water is deeper. Close to one of the inlet streams. Close to the spot where, many years before, a pregnant cow fell into the marshland that fringed the adjoining pasture land. The rescue took many hours and much manpower. Wishing to avert a repeat of the event, the farmer decided to dig down and create a pool. Cowslip Pool.

The glare on the surface makes it difficult for me to see into the depths, but eventually my eyes adjust and the rich weed growth that carpets the bed becomes evident. I know this is a regular haunt of one of the large brown trout that have thrived in the pool since their introduction as ten-inch fish several years ago. I continue to study the water, but see nothing. I put on a Daddy Long-Legs and dap it under the rod tip, no more than eighteen inches from the bank. As I twitch the fly on the surface, it generates small ripples, gently spreading across the surface - betraying its presence. Without warning, the surface erupts as a huge white gape engulfs the fly. Instinctively, I set the hook and a battle of instinct versus blind faith ensues...

As I release the fish, I guesstimate its weight at somewhere between five and six pounds - testament to the quality of the pool.

That Trout was special in many ways, but it's capture was also particularly poignant. I believe it was the last big brownie to be captured before Cowslip Pool ceased to be run by the trout fishing syndicate I had been part of for many years. A variety of events conspired to make the syndicate financially unviable and, although I retained the lease myself, for the last year, the pool was hardly fished.

Then, fate intervened. During a fishing trip with Fennel, the conversation drifted towards his seemingly futile quest to secure a water which could become a sanctuary for Wild Carp – somewhere the strain could be protected, nurtured, studied and occasionally fished for. A meeting was arranged with the owners, who were particularly keen on the conservation aspect of the proposal, and the pool was secured. This then provided the impetus to move forward with the Wild Carp Trust - a concept that had been gestating for some time.

I don't pretend to be a carp fisherman, having caught only a few over the years. But I am aware I owe a huge debt to that carp which captivated me as a child, and led me down a path that enriched my life in many ways. A wild carp on the fly is a sublime experience. I believe that securing Cowslip for the protection of Wild Carp goes some way to repaying this debt.

Some say fishing ruined me. I say fishing *made* me.

Portrait of the angler as a young man!

A Cowslip Brown

The start of the day…

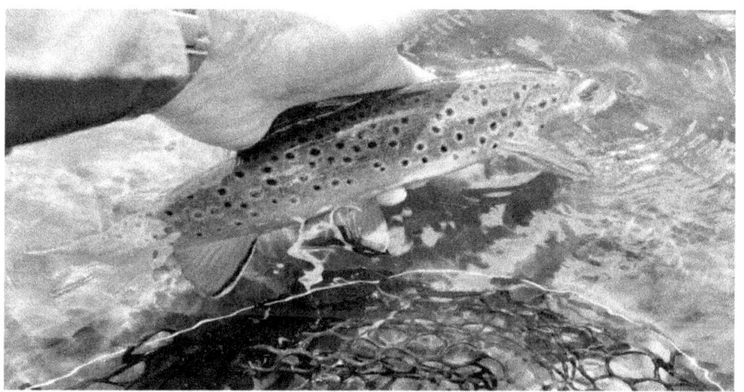

Welsh Gold

A Scourie Loch; close to heaven.

Home of the "Boomerang Trout"

Irish fly-caught Bass

A fly-caught Wild Carp